Rob, Dom and Mikey were fed up with the corporate treadmill. When they decided to change careers, they looked for a website to help them escape – except there wasn't one. So they started their own. Three years later and they have started a movement called Escape the City. Over 100,000 people have joined www.escapethecity.org in pursuit of exciting and unconventional careers. They are the first online start-up in the world to raise more than £500,000 in investment equity crowdfunding – and they did this entirely from their own membership.

The Escape Manifesto is the book that the guys wish they had read three years ago on the London Underground when they were commuting back and forth from their corporate cubicles. It is an inspirational call to action, packed with practical advice and encouragement. If you work in a corporate job that doesn't make you tick and you have ever wondered whether there is more to life, this book is for you. Step off the corporate treadmill – find an exciting job, start your own business, or go on a big adventure. Stop dreaming, start planning and do something different!

D1099138

"*The Escape Manifesto* is a wonderful resource for anyone looking to move away from the corporate world and into a job they love. From the whys to the whats to the hows, this guide will help you take that leap once and for all."
Alexis Grant, Entrepreneurial Writer and Managing Editor of *Brazen Life*

"Not only does *The Escape Manifesto* provide an essential step-by-step guide to breaking out of the corporate world and pursuing a more meaningful career, but it also shows you that you are not alone in your quest for a more fulfilling life and that the fears you may have are natural and symptomatic of the society within which we live. *The Escape Manifesto* really is a must-read for anyone sitting in their cubicle daydreaming about what else could be."
Chris Mooney, Ex-IBM, Ex-Citigroup

"Most people don't know why they're doing what they're doing. They imitate others, go with the flow, and follow paths without making their own. These guys get it – that's why the world needs *The Escape Manifesto*."
Derek Sivers, Founder of CD Baby and Author of *Anything You Want*

"I consider Mike, Rob and Dom as trusted peers and collaborators in our joint mission to lay a clear, secure and viable path for corporate employees who want to leave and start a business. Their advice is sound, and their experience is based on success in the real world. Buy the book!"
Pamela Slim, Author of *Escape from Cubicle Nation*

"*The Escape Manifesto* provides practical and fully relatable advice to help anyone explore the notion that their work life can be more fulfilling. If you feel stuck and helpless, just commit to one thing – read this book. Everyone has a choice to find joy in their work; Rob, Dom, and Mikey have conveniently paved the road towards that."
Julie Clow, Author of *The Work Revolution*

"*The Escape Manifesto* is a call-to-action for all unfulfilled corporate drones – open your eyes to the universe of opportunities, be brave and make the leap of faith into the unknown. You will not regret it!"
Guy Livingstone, Co-founder and President of Tough Mudder

"*The Escape Manifesto* is that extra push of encouragement most of us need to disrupt our traditional patterns of thought, in order to get what we really want out of our careers, relationships and lives."
Rachael Chong, Founder of Catchafire

"Do as they say and do as they do. These guys have the keys to the chain that's keeping you locked to your desk. Time to escape."
Jeff Jarvis, Author of *What Would Google Do?*

"In a world of conformists we need organisations who are prepared to do things differently. How many other start-ups would turn down venture capital in order to raise £600,000 from their own members? An important book for anyone interested in stepping off the treadmill."
Darren Westlake, Crowdcube

"Our minds can be our worst enemies when it comes to making big life decisions. The important thing to remember is that we aren't meant to 'find ourselves' . . . it is through action that we create ourselves. *The Escape Manifesto* is a potent reminder of the power

of initiative over procrastination. Do something. Start by reading this book. But to change your life, then go out and do something different!"
Rob Archer, Founder of The Career Psychologist

"So many of us end up following conventional career paths without being aware of the alternatives. It is so easy to get stuck climbing the corporate ladder. Read this book, plan your transition, and then make a positive change for yourself. Or don't, and in 10 years' time you'll always think 'what if'!"
Frank Yeung, Ex-Investment Banker, Founder of Poncho 8

"*The Escape Manifesto* makes excuses for not changing the status quo in your career strangely disappear. You've been warned, if you read this book, stuff will happen. I also met my wife at the launch party of Escape the City. These guys have all the answers."
Ben Keene, Social Entrepreneur, Founder of Tribewanted

"The world is filled with potentially brilliant people living mediocre lives; anyone who says that this is how it has to be deserves to be whacked around the head with this book."
Dave Cornthwaite, Adventurer

"This is a fantastic resource for anyone wanting to step off the treadmill and make a big change in their life. Great to see a book that is down-to-earth, easy to navigate and doesn't preach. It will prove just the catalyst and enabler that so many people need to help them on their way."
Sarah Outen, Ocean Rower, Adventurer

"Seriously inspirational. A revolutionary handbook for the unfulfilled workers of the world."
Roman Krznaric, Author of *How to Find Fulfilling Work* and Co-Founder of The School of Life

"People often say to me: 'I wish I could do what you do'. The correct answer is, of course, that they can. They just don't think they can. Here is a book aimed at turning that wish into a reality."
Alastair Humphreys, Adventurer, Author, Speaker

"Darwin actually advised us that those who survived weren't the fittest, but the most adaptable. As industrialism winds down many more of us are realising that the old boxes no longer work, neither emotionally or economically. The Escape team have distilled the special sauce that will help those willing to be defined not by what they own but by what they create to live lives of passion, authenticity and (crucially) have a lot of fun doing it. The world is shifting. Ride the wave. Escape the City."
Mark Stevenson, Founder of The League of Pragmatic Optimists, Author of *An Optimist's Tour of the Future*

"If I'd had this book years ago, I would have spared myself a lot of agonising and heartache. Rob and Dom have a no-nonsense approach that is grounded in the reality of their own escape and having helped thousands of others to step off the travelator. If you have suddenly woken up in a job you're not sure you should be in, this book is a no-brainer."
Tom Rippin, Founder of On Purpose (Ex-McKinsey)

Registered office
Capstone Publishing Ltd. (A Wiley Company), John Wiley and Sons Ltd, The Atrium, Southern Gate, Chichester, West Sussex, PO19 8SQ, United Kingdom

For details of our global editorial offices, for customer services and for information about how to apply for permission to reuse the copyright material in this book please see our website at www.wiley.com.

Library of Congress Cataloging-in-Publication Data
Symington, Rob, 1983–
    The escape manifesto : quit your corporate job, do something different! / Rob Symington.
        pages cm
    Includes bibliographical references and index.
    ISBN 978-0-85708-362-3 (pbk.)
    1. Career changes.   2. Career development.   3. Job satisfaction.   I. Title.
    HF5384.S96 2013
    650.14–dc23
                                    2013011057

A catalogue record for this book is available from the British Library.

ISBN 978-0-857-08362-3 (paperback)   ISBN 978-0-857-08370-8 (ebk)
ISBN 978-0-857-08364-7 (ebk)   ISBN 978-0-857-08363-0 (ebk)

Set in 10/13 pt MyriadPro-Regular by Toppan Best-set Premedia Limited

Printed in Great Britain by TJ International Ltd, Padstow, Cornwall, UK

CAPSTONE
A Wiley Brand

THE ESCAPE MANIFESTO

Life is short. Quit your corporate job. Do something different!

escape the city

WILEY

CONTENTS LIST

THE ESCAPE MANIFESTO

All our life we jump through hoops.
Often without asking why.
It's easy to feel stuck – a small cog in a big machine.
It doesn't have to be like this.
Don't waste your life living someone else's.
Don't wait for permission.
Life is too short to do work that doesn't matter to you.
Want your memoirs to be worth reading?
Make your choices your own. Be brave. Be inquisitive.
Stop using lack of money or experience as an excuse.
You don't have to risk it all to explore new options.
You owe it to yourself to find work that makes you tick.
Our world is changing. Careers are changing.
Take advantage or keep your head down. You choose.
The winners are building lives on their own terms.
Take small leaps. Meet people. Ask for help. Save. Plan.
Change jobs. Build businesses. Go on BIG adventures.
Start Something You Love. It's not easy. Push. Sweat.
No one ever changed the world by toeing the line.
You are capable of more than you realize.
This is no dress rehearsal. Make it count.
There will never be a perfect time.
And the first step is often the hardest.
So Stop Dreaming and Start Planning.
Do Something Different!

INTRODUCTION

It was another dreary Monday morning. Rob's alarm clock rang off the table. It was still dark outside. He jammed himself into a tube filled with fellow commuters. Everyone adhered to the silent pact of the London Underground; no one looks anyone else in the eye, nobody speaks. A mass of professionals collectively bracing themselves for the week ahead.

Reaching work, Rob (still waking up) tried not to get engaged in conversation in the elevator. He reached his allotted grey cubicle, opened Microsoft Excel and took a deep breath. At that exact moment Dom poked his head over the cubicle wall and whispered: *"this is pretty rubbish isn't it!?"* Rob immediately saw a kindred spirit. Someone else not prepared to settle, someone else bold enough to want more than a sensible job in a big organization.

We were two management consultants with no business-building experience and limited capital who came up with an idea that excited us so much it just wouldn't go away. It is an idea that has now seen us quit our jobs and spend the last three years building a global community of over 100,000 people who also believe that life is too short to do work that doesn't matter to them.

Every day we get emails from people in different cities around the world saying "WE NEED THIS HERE!" Although our idea was born in "The City"

(London's financial heartland) we have discovered that it resonates far beyond the UK in many different industries and countries. This is a widespread phenomenon – more and more people working in big organizations, over-burdened with process and bureaucracy, are asking themselves whether they can expect more from their careers.

We have now been joined by a third partner, Mikey, who escaped an investment bank to help us set up our HQ in New York. Mikey is another comrade in the fight to save people (and ourselves) from the corporate treadmill. The more people we speak to, the more we realize what a massive problem this is. So many talented and passionate people doing work that doesn't really matter to them.

We are three normal people who were treading the conventional path through the world of big organizations and corporate jargon – doing work that didn't really make us tick. You'll see our story threaded throughout the book. However, if you've ever thought to yourself – "surely there's more to life than this job?" – then this is your story too.

*   *   *

We are writing this book at a time when global capitalism is in crisis. Everywhere institutions and governments are struggling to cope with environmental, social and political challenges, technological innovation, and increased people power. Everywhere we read about surveys telling us that job dissatisfaction is worryingly high. Doctors talk about an epidemic of anxiety and depression in developed countries.[1]

The way things work isn't working.

We are, at the start of the 21st century, faced with huge challenges and even bigger opportunities. And yet, paralyzed by fear or a perceived lack of viable alternatives, so many of us keep our heads down and keep treading the conventional path.

The world is changing. Companies that dominated markets two decades ago don't even exist today. People are doing jobs in today's economy that hadn't been invented ten years ago. Even five years ago we wouldn't have been able to build our business in the way that we are today. Not changing in a world where change is accelerating is a very dangerous approach. It is far too easy for us to laugh at the Kodaks and Blockbusters of this world as being examples of organizations that failed to evolve without realizing that the same will be true for us as individuals if we fail to adapt.

If you are anything like us before we escaped, you may be noticing a vast mismatch between the things you are interested in and the realities of your job. In our case, we were fascinated by the power of the Internet to mobilize people behind an idea. We loved reading about how new technologies were challenging goliaths in every industry and disrupting the status quo. And yet, there we were, working in massive organizations that *were the status quo*. They of all places were unlikely to be the ones shaping the future – they represent the past. Our corporate jobs weren't plugged into the world we wanted to be working in. We left when we realized that it would always be this way.

We have spent the last three years thinking about why so many of us end up doing work that doesn't matter to us and questioning what can be done about it. Our personal experiences have been invaluable, but even more enlightening have been the countless conversations with people who aspire to lead a life on their own terms.

You will read many of their stories in this book. No two escapes are the same. There is no guidebook for building an unconventional career. However, there are certain themes that unite people who have stepped off the corporate treadmill. We have identified nine broad ideas embodied by people who successfully "escape the city". If we were doctors diagnosing corporate job dissatisfaction then these nine ideas would form the basis of our cure:

Idea 1. Change = opportunity

Whenever there have been big shifts in human civilization (think the shift from subsistence to agriculture or from agriculture to industry) two big things have happened:

1. People get hurt (usually those who fail to adapt and therefore became obsolete).

2. Some people profit greatly (usually those who understand the changes and are in a position to take advantage of them).

Those of us who will prosper and enjoy ourselves in the coming years will be those who embrace change rather than resist it. Throughout the book we'll look at why understanding change is crucial if you want to thrive in the economy of the future – especially if you're planning on building a career on your own terms rather than being "owned" by a big corporation.

Idea 2. People are opportunities

Most people who do genuinely exciting jobs in progressive organizations didn't find their opportunity on a job board. You cannot underestimate the importance of building genuine relationships with people doing interesting work in areas that interest you. We'll also look at why your next opportunity will probably come via someone you haven't yet met in your extended social and professional circle and what you can do to help this process.

Idea 3. Develop skills – stop chasing qualifications

The established career dogma tells you to spend up to ten years in academic institutions getting qualifications to equip you to do your chosen career. In many sectors this is important and in some it is crucial (think engineer, doctor, pilot). However, far too many of us study for that liberal arts degree, that masters or that MBA without necessarily knowing why – other than it seeming like a "sensible thing to do". In the process, we get ourselves into debt (limiting our options) and delay the far more important activity of experiencing lots of things in order to work out what we want to do with our lives. In this book, we argue that the agile, employable workers of the future get ahead through learning by doing, targeting specific skills and teaching themselves things that interest them.

Idea 4. Just start – doing beats thinking every time

Successful escapees often talk of engineering serendipity. What they mean is that, through being proactive, they are making things happen for themselves. You are not going to change jobs by thinking about your escape or by complaining that it is hard – you are going to change jobs by taking steps forward (no matter how modest). In this book we argue that you don't have to expose yourself to huge risks to discover new paths. You simply have to take small steps in new directions. It is only through making a habit of "doing" that you will be able to manufacture a transition for yourself that doesn't involve a blind leap of faith.

Idea 5. Information is power – be inquisitive

We wouldn't be writing this book if we hadn't been inquisitive about the future and our place within it. We would still be sitting in our corporate cubicles wondering where to find exciting opportunities. Access to information has been radically democratized by the Internet. There is no longer an excuse for not knowing about something that interests you. You will not be able to take advantage of opportunities that cross your path if you don't understand them. Innovation often happens when ideas from dramatically different areas cross-fertilize. The more ideas you engage with, the more you are putting yourself in a position to spot new and exciting opportunities.

Idea 6. Dealing with fear and risk

Fear and worry are incredibly useful emotions. Being fearful of something that may harm you means you are protecting yourself from potential harm. Worrying about things that might happen allows you to plan and mitigate potential risks. However, you live in a body that evolved for a very different reality to today's society. Often fear causes us to run away from things to avoid short-term pain when the long-term result would have been favourable. This is particularly powerful with big career decisions. A basic understanding of your mind can equip you to better distinguish between useful and useless fear and potentially free you from the cycle of analysis and paralysis.

Idea 7. Set your own principles

You are surrounded by opportunities to rank yourself against other people. Like it or not, you subconsciously compare yourself to your friends and colleagues on a ladder of achievement. It is human nature.

Through the media, society's norms and your parents you have developed a definition of success. If you live in a city you are constantly surrounded by people who are better or worse off than you. Faced with this barrage of cues it is really hard to remember what you personally enjoy doing and find the space to develop your own definitions of success. Knowing your principles is crucial for making good career decisions as they provide you with a lens through which you can assess and identify new opportunities.

Over the coming chapters we will explore why "following your passion" is like trying to find the pot of gold at the end of the rainbow. If you wait to find that one job where your passions are fully reflected in the work you may be waiting some time. Passions don't tend to map to job titles (or companies, or whole industries). Instead, we argue, you should follow your principles, work on things that interest you and strive to solve problems that you care about. Through doing so, you will allow your passions to express themselves.

Idea 8. See any Escape as a startup

When you are starting a business your plan will depend on certain assumptions and you will need to mitigate certain risks. You will have a certain amount of investment and you will need to closely manage the amount of cash coming into the business against the amount flowing out. Your career transition, even if you're not starting a business, is remarkably similar. There is a lot of fluffy career advice out there. We believe that seeing your career change as a startup is an effective way of consistently dealing with uncertainty whilst managing risk until you find the way that works. This approach encourages you to create a vision, define your principles, map your assumptions, and manage your risks whilst you figure out the right direction.

Idea 9. "Do something different" as a strategy for everything

Standing out is scary. You risk being laughed at. You risk being wrong. In the industrial age corporations needed people who could fit in, people who could follow instructions, people who would stay firmly in the box. Today's economy needs people who are prepared to stand out. If you aren't remarkable (literally "worth remarking on") you'll be squeezed out in the inevitable race to the bottom (faster, cheaper, outsourced). Until you do something different your CV looks exactly like thousands of others. Compared to your parent's generation there are far more capable and over-qualified people today chasing the best gigs. The best way to give yourself a competitive advantage in your career isn't to collect qualifications until someone picks you . . . it is to consistently operate differently to your competition in order to get noticed by people who value innovation, creativity and bravery.

* * *

The three of us have written this book to talk you through what we've learnt. This book isn't based on academic theories. It's based on our experience, the experiences of the hundreds of people we've met who have built lives on their own terms, and the thousands of conversations we've had with corporate professionals desperate to escape but stuck on the eternal question: "If not this, then what?"

This is the book we wish we had read when we were planning our own escapes. It is a book for anyone who wants to live a life on their own terms outside of the corporate mainstream. It is not an instruction manual because the process is different for everyone. Part of the reason why we took so long to make the leap is that we were looking for step-by-step guidance where there can be none. We had spent so long on the assembly line of our education and careers and had become so used to following instructions that we were scared to put ourselves in positions where a) we might fail and b) we might have to make big decisions for ourselves.

This book is for you if you've found yourself in a job that looks great on paper but just doesn't satisfy you. This book is for you if you've always done what is expected of you and played by the rules and have begun thinking that there must be more to life. This book may upset you if you don't like being told that with hard work and a different approach you can build a different life and career for yourself. Or if you believe work is something to be endured, that there is no other way, and that anyone who does otherwise is rich or cheating.

We hope that this book provides an element of support, comfort and inspiration for the uncertainty and exhilaration that comes with building a life on your own terms away from the suffocating blanket of jobs in big corporates. This is your invitation to stop dreaming, start planning and do something different with your life.

As with anything in life, use what is useful, reject what is not and make your decisions your own. If you have been feeling stuck then we hope these pages will be useful. We don't have all the answers. We do have lots of questions. We hope you use this book to figure out some answers that are truly yours.

You are at the start of a search for something better. Let the hunt terrify and excite you. This is what life is about. The process is the journey. Don't obsess about the end point. Enjoy the ride. There is no such thing as universal truth – we are all so different. Find your own truth and leave the rest of the world to search for theirs.

Good luck and please do let us know how you get on.

Rob, Dom and Mikey
Escape the City
London, 2013
www.escapethecity.org

PS. Our members often refer to "Escape the City" as "Esc" or "Escape". We will use similar naming conventions through the book.

PART ONE

PRE-ESCAPE

CHAPTER 1

THE TRAVELATOR

A cold but sunny London day, April 2009. We are eating our lunch on the steps of St Pauls Cathedral; enjoying a few brief moments of fresh air watching the old No.9 Routemaster Double Decker Buses drive down Fleet Street before we have to return to our spreadsheets and PowerPoint presentations.

The conversation returns, as it often does these days, to our corporate jobs. We are grappling with these questions: Why are our jobs so unfulfilling? How did we end up here? Are we crazy if we no longer want to work here? And, crucially: What can we do about it?

But the sensible voices in our heads are saying:

"Don't complain. This is what real-life is like."
"At least we've got jobs; many people would love these jobs."

We used to spend a lot of time pondering these questions. It's very easy to feel like you're being ungrateful, immature or naïve. However, the more we analyzed our situations, the more we realized that the path that had led us to the corporate world had been semi-automatic at best. Were we to resign, mad as it sounds, we felt it would be the first truly active decision we had ever taken.

We felt like we were being carried along by an invisible force. A force with its own agenda, values and definitions of success. We call this force "The Travelator".

> *DEFINITION The Travelator (N):*
>
> *The conventional path that most graduates and professionals find themselves on. A path that starts in school and university and can continue right until retirement. The Travelator implies a level of conformity and passivity. Stepping off The Travelator is hard. It's hard enough to notice that you are even on it.*

Ask yourself two questions, two questions that you have no doubt asked on many occasions when your evening plan evaporates into thin air as you are yet again required to stay late to work on a seemingly important task:

Question 1: Why am I working for this organization?
Question 2: Am I crazy if I don't want to be here?

The problem is that the decision-making process that got you to where you are today may not have been entirely your own. Often the values of your work environment don't reflect your own. Often it's easier to inherit external definitions of success than it is to cultivate your own.

We reasoned that it was more important to focus on what we *did* want to do rather than wallow in the negatives of what we didn't. However, we also realized that you do need to understand what you don't like in order to discover what could make you tick.

How can you avoid your enemy if you can't even identify him?

Open your eyes. You are on a Travelator.

Walk it knowingly or get off.

Manny:	I want the weekend off. I want a life.
Bernard:	This is life! We suffer and slave and expire. That's it!
Manny:	We have needs! Fran wants to learn the piano, I want some time to myself, you want to go out with a girl ...
Bernard:	Don't make me laugh ... bitterly. Fran will fail, you'll toil your life away, and I'll die alone, upside down on the floor of a pub toilet.

Dylan Moran and Bill Bailey – Black Books[1]

WHY DOES THIS WORLD NOT WORK FOR SO MANY OF US?

"I don't want my memoirs to be like reading a compliance manual – a history of the rules and regulations of my corporate confinement. I don't want to wear my suit anymore; I don't want to shave.

I don't want my alarm to go off at 5:30am anymore. I feel tired, pale and fat. I have gained little from this punishment.

The underlying constant has been my lack of enthusiasm for the constraints on my creativity. I can't think or make decisions without them being suppressed by standard operating procedures.

It's actually so bad that when you try to brainstorm, you need to snap out of it before you can open your mind up. I've been institutionalized into not thinking. The Thought Police have got to me.

The corporate behemoths of yesterday are stuck in their old ways. They have become factories, places to do business and make money, not places to inspire and change lives.

Either work for someone whose ideas of business, environment and philosophy are aligned with yours, set up your own business/community, or just carry on and let the 'what ifs' pile up until you retire and are too old to do the things you once dreamed of."

Mikey Howe, writing to himself two months before deciding to escape from the investment bank he worked in to become Escape the City's New York partner

We are our jobs

Before we escaped, Rob found himself at an awkward British drinks party. A girl engaged him in conversation. Within seconds, inevitably, she asked him what he did. When he responded "I'm a management consultant" she said "don't take this the wrong way" – as if there was a right way to take it – "but you look like one".

Rob promptly went home, shaved his head and resolved to quit his job. It wasn't that he minded looking like a management consultant; it was that he minded *being* a management consultant.

In the past, for most people, a job was just a means to an end – a tool to support your family and guarantee a certain level of income. A job was a necessary requirement to survive.

Today many of us have loftier ideals. We want our work to provide us with some form of meaning or fulfilment beyond the simple process of earning money in order to afford to exist. For many of us our career and our jobs are our highest form of self-expression.

Today most of us feel like our jobs are inextricably linked to who we feel we are as people. The polite question "what do you do?" is far more than an enquiry into how you earn your living. It feels like being asked "who are you?"

So, if your job forms a large part of your identity and sense of self-worth, and you don't enjoy it, then it's little wonder that you also feel pretty miserable about yourself and your life when you try and answer that question.

> ❝ *Inevitably, your career will define you, and then you'll be left to contend with whether you like yourself defined that way or not. That, I think, is what makes corporate jobs frustrating and scary. I don't want to be defined by my blazer and high heels.* ❞
>
> **Denice – Escape the City Member, Philippines**

The emperor's new clothes

Hans Christian Andersen tells the story of how a fabulously rich, powerful and egotistical emperor is promised a new suit of clothes by two weavers. The clothes are meant to be invisible to those unfit for their positions – stupid or incompetent. When the Emperor parades in front of his subjects in his new clothes a child cries out, "But he isn't wearing anything at all!"

When we worked in the corporate world we found that it was easy to be impressed by job titles and salaries without knowing whether any real value was being created. For the past decade hedge fund managers have been the celebrities of the finance world. They are seen as alchemists who make money when the markets go up or down. It's all too easy to say "oh that's impressive" and keep quiet for fear of seeming stupid if you don't know how they work.

We resolved that we weren't prepared to work in jobs that were considered high-powered and successful if the reality was far from the truth. We decided that the actual daily reality of our jobs was far more important to us than what other people thought about them.

 The work was considered glamorous but was intellectually and emotionally unsatisfying, physically exhausting, and spiritually draining. That was my life. The long hours in my cubicle under fluorescent light left no time, and no emotional energy, for deep relationships. I was lonely and tired…

Andreas Kluth – ex-investment banker, author of "Hannibal and Me, How I conquered my banking job" at Salon.com[2]

Politics and bullshit

Why is it so hard to be yourself at work? People who work in big corporations often don't speak like normal human beings. We caught the bug ourselves and ended up using ridiculous expressions like "let's get our ducks in a row" and talking about things like "capacity", "learnings" and "leverage".

It seemed like no one at work was really being themselves. We desperately wanted to be able to be ourselves in that environment. Talking in anything louder than a whisper in the open plan cubicle farm on the 9th floor used to attract strange looks from our fellow inmates as if to say: "What are those guys doing over there? They're not TALKING are they?!"

We weren't comfortable with the people that we became in our corporate offices. Sure it was still *us*, but we wanted to be able to bring our whole selves to work. And, despite being confident people, we found that those grey walls made it very hard to let ourselves be ourselves there – not some "Stepford Wife" version of our characters designed to fit into a preconceived idea of "how you should behave".

It is often reported that the people who get ahead in the corporate world aren't those who are best at their jobs, but those who are good at politics and "playing the game". We know that that's "just life". You know that's "just life". However, it's up to you whether you want to work in such an environment. Do you want to work in a world where appearances, perceptions and presentation carry more weight than output, execution and how nice a person you are?

> 66 *If you had to identify, in one word, the reason why the human race has not achieved, and never will achieve, its full potential, that word would be 'meetings'.*
>
> **Dave Barry – columnist, author**

Autonomy, mastery, purpose

It was 28 April 2008 and Manchester United (one of Rob's true loves) were playing Barcelona in the European Cup semi-finals that evening. The football fans amongst you will appreciate the pain of this story. The rest of you, just imagine that you were planning to spend your evening doing something really important to you!

Throughout the afternoon Rob had worked furiously on a particular presentation in order to leave the office at a reasonable hour and watch the game with his friends. As evening approached there was still no sign of the director who had asked for the piece of work. His manager suggested that they should wait for him to return from a meeting and review the work together before going home for the day.

So they waited, and waited, and waited. A couple of brief text messages arrived alerting them to the fact that the director was held up in his meeting. 7 pm turned to 9 pm and still they waited. Eventually, at 10 pm a phone call came through saying that they had better catch up in the morning.

The worst thing about the whole experience wasn't that Rob missed the game, it was that it transpired that there was no pressing deadline for that piece of work and the client never saw the presentation in the end. For someone who likes working hard on something worth achieving this was incredibly frustrating.

A small loss in the scheme of things (there will be other semi-finals no doubt) but this story neatly encompasses how three really important ingredients for fulfilling work were missing from our corporate jobs:

1. We didn't have control over our day-to-day lives.

2. We weren't developing skills that we valued.

3. And so much of the work we sweated over just didn't seem to matter.

Dan Pink writes some extremely interesting analysis on the psychology of work in his book *Drive – the Surprising Truth About What Motivates Us.*

We consider it recommended reading for anyone interested in understanding the drivers behind job (dis)satisfaction. In the book he highlights three crucial ingredients for fulfilling work:

1. **Autonomy** – the desire to direct your own life.

2. **Mastery** – the urge to get better and better at something that matters to you.

3. **Purpose** – the yearning to do what you do in the service of something larger than yourself.

Take a moment to reflect on whether your current job provides you with a significant amount of any of these ingredients. Is it any wonder you're unfulfilled if it doesn't allow you any of them?

No wonder you're not feeling satisfied with your career if the only autonomy you have is during your evenings and weekends, the only thing you're mastering is the art of looking busy or Microsoft Excel and the only purpose you have in your life is reaching the weekend.

Dave Mayer left his project manager job at Cisco to start an innovative water bottle company in northern California. He told us that he wanted to be in control of his own destiny: "I didn't want to have a boss who was telling me to do something, who was told by his boss, who was told by his boss."

Nina Elvin-Jensen escaped from being an investment property agent to set up littledelivery.com, a website selling children's presents. She explained how unfulfilling she found the monotonous working routine: "I knew I was just a small cog in a large money-making machine."

By contrast, Rob Cornish was a fund manager who enjoyed his job but hated the 9-to-5 regime (which he said was more like 7-to-7). In his own words: "Financial success is great but freedom of lifestyle and being able to plan your own day is really incredibly important too."

Just like the examples above, we wanted to love our work and have the freedom to do it on our own terms. We had none of these three ingredients in our corporate jobs. We decided to leave when we realized it would always be that way.

People who spend a lot of time on task forces, leading multiple-day offsite meetings and generating enormous binders and decks of PowerPoint slides, often have sober moments when they think, 'What in heaven's name does this have to do with the real world?'

***Pamela Slim* – Escape from Cubicle Nation**

Warning – your health may suffer

We would occasionally find out that the men and women at the top of our organization were only about ten years older than us. We weren't concerned that they had risen so high in so few years. We were absolutely terrified because we had assumed they were as old as our parents. If this is what working in the corporate world does to your physical health, forget it – we didn't want to know!

We're sure you can relate to the rushed sandwich lunches eaten "Al Desko", the sleepy afternoons powered on caffeine and sugar, the days where you arrive at work as the sun is rising and leave way after sunset. Throw in a couple of hangovers a week and not enough time for exercise and you have the perfect cocktail for an extremely unhealthy lifestyle with low resistance to stress.

Your body isn't designed for spending all day sitting down, staring at a screen in an air-conditioned room with windows that don't open. Do you have a sore back or neck? Check out http://www.onlineuniversity.net/work-is-murder/ for some scary statistics. It is sadly ironic how the activity that you're performing to earn money to survive could end up being the thing that ruins you.

Your job may be affecting your health.

Don't let it.

> *I found myself changing into a different person as the years went by. I started developing phobias and I was frequently tired and/or ill.*
>
> **Keith Jenkins – ex-investment banker, travel blogger**

`esc` Corporate creativity is an oxymoron

Piers Calvert used to be an exotic equity derivatives trader at Deutsche Bank in London. After five years he quit, leaving for South America. Today he works as a photographer living in Bogotá, Colombia. The corporate world simply wasn't creative enough for him. He knew this when he realized that he put more effort into the layout and colours of the spreadsheets he was building than into managing the billions of Euros of risk that they represented.

If you should be sure of one thing in life it's that nothing ever stays the same. And yet, big organizations aren't necessarily the best models of organization for quick response to changing circumstances. As we've already indicated, we experienced a massive mismatch between the exciting and entrepreneurial world of business innovation, technology and enterprise that we were reading about online and the reality of our jobs.

Charles Leadbeater, a researcher at the London think tank Demos, delivered a fascinating TED talk[3] where he explained how "big corporations have an inbuilt tendency to reinforce past success". Clay Shirky, who writes about the effects of Internet on society, goes further, saying how "institutions will always try to preserve the problem to which they are the solution".

You shouldn't expect your employer to evolve towards a more progressive workplace if the way they have been operating has served them well (as far as they are concerned) so far. Many of us work in companies that have been around for decades and, whilst some are evolving, many still have the kind of company culture that just doesn't vibe with the way you want your working life to be.

The problem in working for a big institution is that it necessarily takes away one's ability to be impulsive and think freely because the bosses don't like it. You can't go around spontaneously taking big risks every day, mixing things up unannounced. They love to say you can but you really can't. So you have to first leave this environment in order to regain your ability to respond spontaneously to your own impulses.

Piers Calvert – Exotics trader turned exotic photographer

Institutions and leaders are failing us

Robert Peston, the BBC's business editor, probably had the greatest insight into the unravelling of the global economy that started with the credit crunch. His recent book, *How Do We Fix This Mess?*, opens with a scene on the trading floor of a large investment bank being briefed on "collateralised debt obligations" and "credit default swaps".

By his own admission, he was finding it incredibly difficult to understand what the trader was talking about. And, as Alison Roberts writes in the Evening Standard,[4] "if Peston, with almost 30 years' experience of City jargon wasn't getting it, then who on earth was?"

Most of us have been brought up to respect our elders and to defer to people with more experience, knowledge or – frankly – power than us. The past few years have shown that our leaders (from politicians to businesspeople to regulators to journalists) can't always be trusted to have our best interests at heart. Or, if they do, then they are too incompetent to manage significant risks on behalf of the rest of the population.

It's easy to bemoan the lesser sides of human nature – greed, deceit and shortsightedness – when thinking of the very human failings of the corporate world. It's far too easy to point to scandals at Enron, UBS and Barclays or even individual "mavericks" like Bernie Madoff and say that they represent a greater rottenness in the system. The "we-live-in-a-time-of-titanic-institutional-failure" story is a sensationalist one for sure, but can you argue with the evidence?

The institutional failures of the past few years are one thing, the examples of how people in your life, and perhaps you yourself, are feeling the pain are even worse. Cuts, redundancies, pension pots evaporating. People who have played by the rules their whole lives have been sold short by "the system". We're not surprised if you're looking at that career path and thinking – "no thanks, I fancy my chances on my own".

Robert Peston's book raises fundamental questions about profit, genuine value and growth: "You fear that a good deal of bank innovation is still about gulling even sophisticated investors into buying stuff they don't understand." When we have one of the UK's leading business analysts saying how "a lot of the growth [the banking sector] achieved was socially useless", we really have to have a real think about what the corporate system is all about and how we see our place in it.

A panel at the 2012 SXSW conference in Texas was organized on the topic of: "Keeping Kids off the Street: Wall Street vs. Startups". Chris Wiggins, an associate professor of applied maths at Columbia University, said he was witnessing graduates rejecting Wall Street in favour of industries where they could "work and profit without bringing their morality under the microscope". "The claim of investment banking that it serves a social purpose by 'lubricating capitalism' has eroded," Professor Wiggins said. "It's simply very difficult for young people to believe that they're serving any social purpose now."

What seems like a popular layman's belief is actually backed up by economists who claim that financial innovation has little productivity benefit. Paul Volcker, once chairman of the US Federal Reserve, claims that there is "little correlation between sophistication of a banking system and productivity growth"[5] and that there is "no neutral evidence that financial innovation has led to economic growth".[6] Paul Krugman, Professor of Economics and International Affairs at Princeton, claims: "the rapid growth in finance since 1980 has largely been a matter of rent-seeking, rather than true productivity."[7]

We certainly didn't feel like we were working in an environment where there was much incentive beyond institutional and personal profit and we didn't feel capable of changing any of this for the better. We believed that proper value was more than just profit. When we realized that the structures of the world we were working in didn't cater to different thinking – we knew that our values were fundamentally at odds with that world.

Corporations respond to the market and to the demands of their shareholders, not to the consciences of their employees.

George Monbiot – Choose Life [8]

WHY DO SO MANY OF US TREAD THIS PATH?

"You're an arts graduate, for heaven's sake.
You didn't want to be a banker anyway.
You wanted to read books and write poetry and kiss girls."

Giles Coren – The Times[9]

We have been taught to be cogs

All the way through our education we are taught to fit in. Obey rules, follow guidance, do homework, meet deadlines. Be quiet. Sit down. Pass tests. Get grades. Eat your vegetables.

The corporate world is remarkably similar. Most organizations want predictable, repeatable, scalable behaviour. They want to tick-off points on recruitment checklists.

> They want someone who meets the spec.
> They want worker bees.
> They want cogs.

We have been taught how to be cogs.

So is it any wonder that when we're faced with the job market for the first time as a graduate we seek out opportunities to return to what we know?

All of us who have trodden the corporate path are people who have learnt how to jump through hoops. This type of traditional education and social conditioning is not helpful if you want to live a life on your own terms – if you want freedom and autonomy.

 Large-scale education was not developed to motivate kids or to create scholars. It was invented to churn out adults who worked well within the system.

Seth Godin – Stop Stealing Dreams

`esc` We make semi-conscious decisions

When we sat down to write this book, Mikey, reflected that he felt like every step prior to his resignation had been pre-programmed into him by school, university and his peer group. Mad as it sounds, he felt that he hadn't once made a proper decision about what to do with his life: "When I realized that all the people that surrounded me at work were in the same boat but were too scared to admit it, I knew I had to escape."

Reflecting on our journeys into the corporate world we realized that the decision to choose our industries and our jobs was barely a conscious one – a lot of chance and randomness was involved. The only reason Rob became a management consultant (in his 16th and final job interview after 15 rejections) was that the guy interviewing him really liked the fact that he had driven an old Land Rover through Africa the year before.

It was so easy to simply react to what was in front of us. The requirement to "just get a sensible job" easily trumped any proper introspection and active decision-making. The realization that many of our decisions hadn't been wholly our own was both terrifying and liberating. Liberating because the question we then had to ask ourselves was: what active decisions might we now take with the rest of our lives?

Matthew McLuckie (great name!) shared a similar thought process with us when recounting how he escaped the world of private equity in order to develop carbon-offsetting projects. He decided that there were two types of people in the corporate world. In Camp 1 he saw people who had long lunches and post-work beers and complained about their jobs a lot. Camp 2 was made up of people who obviously loved what they were doing and had passion and drive.

In his own words: "Having started as an enthusiast in Camp 2, the system gradually wore me down to join the lunch-and-beer club. I found myself getting more irritated with work and knew it was time to leave. You cannot compete with those who love and relish their jobs if your heart is not in it."

We call these people "The Accidentals" (people who got their job because it was a sensible job and it seemed like a good idea at the time).

We were Accidentals.

The corporate world is full of Accidentals. This is such a tragedy. We're talking about educated, passionate, driven people doing work that doesn't matter to them. Are you devoting your precious, all-too-short life to a cause you don't care for? Or to no discernible cause at all?

It is too easy to spend a decade doing a job that you didn't choose for yourself, comforting yourself with the thought that you'll "only do this for a while" before finding what it is that you really want to do with your life.

 So what I saw around me were great kids who had been trained to be world-class hoop jumpers. Any goal you set them, they could achieve. Any test you gave them, they could pass with flying colours. They were, as one of them put it herself, 'excellent sheep'...

William Deresiewicz – in a lecture to the plebe class at the United States Military Academy at West Point, Oct 2009[10]

`esc` The trap of the high achievers

When we were setting up Escape the City in New York we met a banker who admitted that she was probably an alcoholic and that she spent all of her money on clothes to distract herself from how much she hated her job. But she was unwilling to compromise on the salary. She was so used to jumping through the next hoop in the ladder of achievement that she said she was completely clueless as to what else she could do.

That's the same salary that she was splurging on expensive restaurants, booze and high-end couture just to help her deal with the job itself. Is that not absolute madness? Imagine what a large escape fund she could save up in a short amount of time with that cash. She could go travelling for a year. She could start a business. Instead she was stuck in a cycle of consumption and depression.

If you are used to excelling, you usually gravitate towards the jobs where the best and brightest are meant to spend their time. Over the past two decades this has been the professional and financial services sectors – investment banks and corporate law firms.

Often the people who are the unhappiest in their jobs are those who have never failed, who have never dropped a grade. As Rob Archer, the Career Psychologist, said at a recent Escape the City event: "Being relatively clever and very conscientious can be a dangerous combination. It means you'll probably be good at what you do – good enough to get by – but you will also persist and keep trying harder and harder. You will get the job done – but it may be at the expense of your values, health, or even sanity."

It's crazy. You don't think "what do I want to do with my life?" or "where will I be most happy?" You end up thinking "where are all the other high achievers going? I need to be there". If you're used to pegging yourself to society's league table of "success" you'll find that kind of validation in buckets by working for a blue chip corporate. The problem is, for every person who feels genuinely comfortable with their decisions and career path, there are many others who are desperately unhappy but – for a variety of often-complicated reasons – feel completely stuck.

It is very easy to end up being a prisoner of your own high achiever status. Perhaps you should apply the same discipline and focus that has helped you to always succeed to the far greater challenge of developing your own definition of success . . .

 Grads from top schools are funnelled into high-income 80-hour-per-week jobs, and 15–30 years of soul-crushing work has been accepted as the default path. How do I know? I've been there and seen the destruction.

Tim Ferriss – The 4-Hour Work Week

`esc` We don't define success for ourselves

We live in a world that makes it very easy to compare ourselves to others. We have never been more connected, more advertised at, or more aware of what everyone else seems to be achieving. It is very easy to feel bad about your relative failure versus your friend's relative success. It is very easy to adopt other peoples' definitions of success instead of your own.

If you work in a big corporate the chances are you also live in a big city. Big cities are competitive. Everyone is trying to get ahead. Most big city people are "Maximizers" (a word coined by psychologist Barry Schwartz for someone who is always thinking they can do better). These people are generally unhappy.

Add the massive amounts of personal disclosure afforded by Facebook, Twitter and other forms of social media, and you have the perfect cocktail for some seriously confused definitions of success. We live in a world where you can always check out what the next person is doing, achieving or thinking. Our Linkedin notifications ping into our inboxes letting us know when our connections have got new jobs. Now, tell us that's not depressing if you're hunting for an exciting new job!

From this perspective it is no wonder that so many of us struggle to develop personal definitions of success. The holy trinity of 'success' in the corporate environment is power, status and money. It is incredibly hard to see beyond these values when we're spending 5 days a week operating under conditions that are constantly reinforcing them.

We suck in messages from everything from the television, to advertising, to marketing, etc. These are hugely powerful forces that define what we want and how we view ourselves. When we're told that banking is a very respectable profession a lot of us want to go into banking. When banking is no longer so respectable, we lose interest in banking. We are highly open to suggestion. So what I want to argue for is not that we should give up on our ideas of success, but we should make sure that they are our own. We should focus in on our ideas and make sure that we own them, that we are truly the authors of our own ambitions. Because it's bad enough, not getting what you want, but it's even worse to have an idea of what it is you want and find out at the end of a journey, that it isn't, in fact, what you wanted all along.

Alain de Botton – "A kindler, gentler philosophy of success" TED Talk[11]

Most careers advice is so awful

All our lives we are shown a very narrow field of career paths. We are told to get sensible jobs working for big companies. We are told to aspire to job titles – go be a banker, an accountant, a lawyer or a management consultant. Our parents reinforce this direction and it really kicks into overdrive at university where people begin getting generous job offers from big companies – triggering our FOMO ("Fear Of Missing Out").

We are rarely encouraged to consider what might be right for us as individuals. We take obscure personality tests that tell us to be dental hygienists or forensic accountants (no offence if you're either!). We're never told about all the exciting alternatives that are outside the corporate mainstream. The social enterprises, startup companies or exciting businesses where we could actually do work that matters to us.

> 66 *This career path, in other words, is counter-educational. It teaches you to do what you don't want to do, to be what you don't want to be. It is an exceptional person who emerges from this process with her aims and ideals intact. Indeed it is an exceptional person who emerges from this process at all. What the corporate or institutional world wants you to do is the opposite of what you want to do. It wants a reliable tool, someone who can think, but not for herself: who can think instead for the institution.* 99
>
> **George Monbiot – Choose Life**[12]

Conclusion – The Travelator

There is often a contradiction between what you want your job to provide you with (meaning and fulfilment) and what it actually provides you with (income and a sense of security). Of course the latter is desirable – but if you're struggling to enjoy your job, you probably need more of the former. You may find that the most valuable benefit from your time on the Travelator is the realization that you don't want to spend lots of time in that environment after all.

If you are going to make the sacrifices required to work in the corporate world you should at least be sure why you are doing it and what you are getting out of the experience. There should be no illusions about how big organizations operate and, if you decide to stay, no grumbling. Once you've decided it's not for you, enjoy acting on the refreshing realization that your future lies elsewhere.

If escaping a corporate job were easy, you wouldn't be reading this book or feeling stuck. The next chapters explore the powerful forces that can keep you stuck before examining the steps you can take to transition towards an environment where your work might be more enjoyable.

 These prison walls are funny. First you hate 'em, then you get used to 'em. Enough time passes, gets so you depend on them. That's institutionalized. They send you here for life, that's exactly what they take. The part that counts anyways.

Red (Morgan Freeman) – Shawshank Redemption[13]

CHAPTER 2

THOUGHTS AND BLOCKERS

Have you ever heard someone complaining about how something that has happened to them isn't their fault and smiled inwardly to yourself, reflecting that they are the real cause of their own misfortunes? Have you ever heard someone explaining why they can't do something and thought to yourself "these are just excuses"?

We were those people! We told ourselves: "We'll do these jobs for five years and then go do something more interesting/exciting/ entrepreneurial/adventurous/meaningful with our lives." But when push came to shove we felt completely unprepared to make the leap. Worse than that, we came up with a compelling range of reasons why we weren't able to leave our jobs.

In retrospect, *we* were the main thing that was holding us back – all that complaining, all that negativity was simply so many excuses. At the time it was extremely hard to see things objectively. We were particularly good at persuading ourselves why we couldn't change and especially awful at talking ourselves through the reasons why we could.

There were also some real-life realities that were stopping us from resigning – constraints on our options included financial worries and concerns about whether our skills would applicable to new areas. This chapter shares some of the unhelpful thoughts we experienced and, with hindsight, some of the practical blockers that kept us stuck.

It is now much easier for us to analyze the barriers that stopped us from making big career transitions. We have written this chapter to save you from spending as long as we did dithering over your decision to escape. The less time you spend analyzing the pros and cons, the more you can get on with the far more exciting activity of making change happen for yourself.

The first half of this chapter addresses that little voice in your head that tells you to put your escape ideas back on the shelf and carry on with your job. The second half addresses the real-life forces that might keep you stuck.

> *There are two types of people in this world; people who find excuses, and people who find ways through, round, and over their obstacles.*
>
> **Alastair Humphreys – Ten Lessons From The Road**

UNHELPFUL THOUGHTS

"Present fears/Are less than horrible imaginings."

William Shakespeare

"I should be grateful for this job"

All three of us had to face our parents' concerns when we first started talking about resigning from our jobs. And, despite the fact that we are far too old to need permission for these decisions, their opinion that we were turning our backs on a good thing understandably weighed heavily in our minds.

One of the most persuasive reasons we gave ourselves for staying put was that the economy was in such a state that we should just consider ourselves lucky to have a job. It sounded like a very grown-up attitude; we had bills to pay and we kept reading about people losing their jobs.

To get over the "better the devil I know" thoughts, Mikey carried around a post-it note in his wallet with a quote saying: "I'd rather be a failure at something I love than a success at something I hate."

Your employer is buying your time. You are exchanging a certain amount of hours a week for a certain amount of money. If it no longer seems like a bargain worth striking you owe it to yourself to start exploring alternatives, no matter how many people tell you that you should just keep your head down and be grateful for your job.

 Does putting yourself in a position where someone else can turn off all your income just by saying two words ('You're fired') sound like a safe and secure situation to you?

Steve Pavlina[1] – blogger

"I am safe in my current job"

Loyalty is always fragile in the corporate world and especially in a recession. Ask all those employees of Lehman Brothers, masters of the universe in 2007, escorted from the building clutching cardboard boxes in 2008.

Recently many people who have taken conventional career paths, taken no risks, and worked in big corporates all their lives have had it all thrown back in their faces just as they were approaching retirement age. Redundancies, massively reduced pension pots, forced early retirements. When the chips are down we are all expendable.

Brett Veerhusen started his career in finance just as Lehman collapsed. From his new desk he saw employee after employee get fired. Within days he was staring at an empty floor. He told us how they found out about the second round of layoffs through an online finance blog, without a single official word from any of the executives.

Dom and Rob spent a lot of time building spreadsheets on "cost reduction" projects for large corporations. Often a company will leave it to consultants to come in and advise them on becoming more efficient. Why? Because "becoming more efficient" often meant "figuring out to sack". Although we never feared directly for our jobs, we have first-hand experience of how corporate job security is pretty non-existent.

 I was tired of living in fear and being surrounded by such negative energy. When you put 20 people in an office who all are worried about their jobs and their futures, even without any word being voiced, a chill of darkness shrouds the atmosphere. I gave my resignation four hours after the second round of layoffs occurred. If they were going to make adjustments, they may as well account for one more.

Brett Veerhusen – ex-investment banker

"I might damage my career"

Before resigning, Dom wanted to know what impact ending five years as a management consultant might have on his career. He spoke to Clare Johnston, CEO of The Up Group (a London headhunting agency). He asked her about the career implications of trying to start a business and potentially failing.

She responded that it could be nothing but a positive on his CV. If he failed and wanted to get another job in consulting, he would now stand out from all the other candidates with the same degrees and professional experience. What's more, the responsibility and pressure of starting a business would push his experience levels far beyond what he was learning in the more structured corporate environment.

It can be far more dangerous to clock up years in a job where you have no interest in building a long-term career than making a transition that might not work out. This should be a pretty compelling reason to start exploring your options.

> **"** We used to think that Corporate America meant safe, rising jobs, promotions, salaries, life savings, etc. 2008 showed us that was all a lie. Heck, 100,000 people lost their life savings when GM went bust. GM was the most solid company in the world 20 years ago.
>
> **James Altucher – '10 More Reasons You Need To Quit Your Job Right Now'[2]**

"I don't have the right network"

It was very hard to see new opportunities from our desks in the hothouse project rooms in our jobs as management consultants. We knew that many great opportunities came via people but we didn't feel like we had access to the right people.

Our problem was that all our friends were carbon copies of us. No one seemed to have the answer. It was very easy to cruise job boards, talk to headhunters, speak to our friends and conclude that there simply weren't any exciting jobs out there. With hindsight we now know that if you can't find new opportunities you're probably not looking in the right places or actively building relationships with the right people . . . but at the time we felt completely stuck.

Returning to the story of Piers Calvert, the banker who escaped Canary Wharf and now works as a photographer in Bogotá, Colombia. Despite not having a network at all when he moved to South America he completely reinvented himself through the power of networking.

Since escaping he has met the world's smallest man, photographed the president of Colombia, had a G&T with the son of the world's most notorious drug lord Pablo Escobar and set off dynamite in an emerald mine.

It is important to push the boundaries of your network. Later in the book we'll explore some of the ways to meet people who reflect where you want to get to in your career. Stop using not knowing the right people as an excuse!

> *With risk comes reward. I often write to important people out of the blue asking if I can take their picture, and you know, sometimes they say yes, and you suddenly find yourself the next morning in the office of an ex-president having coffee and a chat and taking pictures of him.*

Piers Calvert – Exotics trader turned exotic photographer

"I don't have the right skills"

When we first started thinking about leaving our jobs we had a big enough dose of "Imposter Syndrome" (the feeling that you're always faking it – unable to internalize your accomplishments) without wanting to consider the challenges that would come with leaping into a new industry or job. We fell into the trap of thinking that we didn't have the right skills.

However, we began to realise that most of our skills were pretty generalist and could potentially apply to other working environments (managing people, being organized, building relationships, clear writing and verbal communication, thinking strategically and analytically, managing projects, selling to clients, selling ourselves, negotiating office politics). It would simply be up to us to tell a story to any potential future employer about why we were passionate about what they did and how we could do a good job for them.

Sarah Hilleary was a junior portfolio manager at an investment bank. She knew that she wasn't happy in her job. She had long harboured a dream of starting a business that provided a genuine solution for people. The day she discovered she was gluten intolerant she resolved to start a business providing gluten-free products. The fact that she didn't know how to bake didn't hold her back, she taught herself and the BTempted brand was born.

It's very easy to feel that the process of getting established in a given job, especially if it is a line of work that requires qualifications (like law or accountancy), means that you are committed to that path. Even people who are relatively early on in their careers can feel like it's too late to change – especially when they consider the efforts required to re-establish themselves in a new area.

Jonathan Walter spent 15 years working as an accountant in an investment bank. He started designing furniture for fun and only studied it as a craft when he realized he could turn his passion for design into a career. He now works as a cabinet-maker, making bespoke furniture in North

Cornwall and living ten minutes from some of the best surf on the Cornish coast. Neither Sarah nor Jonathan allowed their lack of skills to hold them back. They did something about it.

There is another factor in your favour. Increasingly, progressive organizations will hire people with track records of "getting stuff done" above any specific checklist of skills.

Tough Mudder, a fast-growing extreme adventures startup in the USA, actively hires people with no experience in the role they are applying for. Their Chief Creative Officer, Alex Patterson, used to be a tax lawyer. Guy, the co-founder (an ex-lawyer) figures that if he can learn any role in less than two years then his employees can do the same. They just need to be smart, passionate and determined.

The more we speak to people who escape corporate jobs, the more we realize that anyone who changes industries or starts a business has had to develop new skills and apply skills from their old job. You can't underestimate the importance of confidence and learning "on the job". Stop underselling yourself. Start backing your ability to adapt.

Study hard what interests you the most in the most undisciplined, irreverent and original manner possible.

Richard P. Feynman – theoretical physicist

esc "I need to have it all figured out"

Here are some of the things we told ourselves whilst justifying why we weren't getting any closer to leaving our jobs:

- "We're waiting for the right business idea . . . "

- "We're waiting to find our dream jobs . . . "

- "We're waiting to discover our passions . . . "

- "We're waiting for the right time . . . "

Waiting is passive and it involves a fundamental misunderstanding about the way the world works. We were like the little boys standing up against the wall in the playground, waiting to be picked for a team. The reality is that in order to *find* new opportunities, *develop* new interests, or *come up* with an exciting business idea you're going to have to **act**.

We had fallen into the trap of thinking that we might wake up one day and "just know" what it is we were meant to do with our lives. Having worked on Escape the City for three years we now realize that this kind of thinking is extremely dangerous because it delays the essential work of taking the required steps to make things happen for yourself.

This is what Steve Jobs was talking about when he said that: "you can't connect the dots looking forward; you can only connect them looking backwards. So you have to trust that the dots will somehow connect in your future."[3]

We were so used to having our futures mapped out (school, degrees, graduate jobs, the corporate career path) that we felt completely under-equipped to start charting a more exciting and unconventional career path.

As you'll see, there's no such thing as a foolproof plan that will carry you through your escape (such a thing is impossible). What you need is the belief that you can start making career decisions based on the key principles that are important to you. The tactics can change but as long as you stay true to your guiding principles you should be able to weather the inevitable ups and downs, uncertainties and triumphs.

The problem with waiting for that "dream job", your "world beating business idea" or a flash of inspiration where you figure out "your calling" is that these things don't really exist in the real world. The main problem with this mentality is that the seemingly rational argument of waiting actually means that you miss out on the many opportunities to meet new people, explore new paths, and discover new situations which are far more suitable to you.

People told us that it wasn't the right time and that we weren't the right people. One day it hit us . . . you'll always either be too young and not have enough experience, savings or contacts or too old and feel that it's too late (married, kids, mortgage).

All you need to do is start the process of working your way through the things that might be holding you back. Often any change is better than no change. Once you accept that there isn't just "one right decision" for your next career move you really take the pressure off. If no one job can realistically satisfy your whole personality, you should stop aiming for it.

Your next job or project just has to tick some of your boxes. You won't do it forever and you'll learn something from the experience whether it is positive or negative. What's important, if you're unhappy, is that you create the forward motion to move yourself from where you are today.

 People have multiple selves. Different jobs will address different parts of ourselves at different periods in our lives [. . .] there's a part that's very pragmatic and there's a part that's very creative, and there are times in life when we give more time and space and energy to one side than the other.

***Herminia Ibarra* – Working Identity**

COMMON BLOCKERS

*"How much better to know that we have dared to
live our dreams than to live our lives in a lethargy of regret."*

Gilbert E. Kaplan – entrepeneur

We are looking for an instruction manual

This second part of the chapter deals with the real blockers that were keeping us stuck in our corporate job (as opposed to the unhelpful thoughts that we covered in the first part).

Why did we freak out when we first considered stepping off The Travelator? Perhaps because we were so used to jumping through society's hoops that we didn't know what to do when the structures of an institution weren't there to direct us towards our next challenge.

There *is* an instruction manual for the conventional life. It involves keeping your head down and doing what you're told. We are probably the most over-qualified and over-educated working generation in the history of humankind. We have access to unprecedented amounts of information and technology. And yet, so many of us are confused about how to navigate any career trajectory that deviates remotely from the well-trodden corporate path.

 There are no magic formulas [. . .] great achievement, deep fulfilment, lasting relationships, or any other aspects of an unquenchably, relentlessly well-lived life aren't formulaically executable or neatly quantifiable. First and foremost, they're searingly, and deeply personally, meaningful. The inconvenient truth is: you'll probably just have to blaze your own trail.

Umair Haque – Harvard Business Review Blog[4]

`esc` We are influenced by other people

We all care what other people think. When a group of your peers are talking about their jobs (it sometimes seems that's ALL anyone talks about these days!) or salaries or promotions you want to feel a sense of validation and self-worth when you talk about what you do.

Lee Strickland spent 14 years running sales and leading creative pitches in media companies. In 2010 she resigned to move to Cornwall with her partner and opened Little Leaf Guest House. She came to some of the very first Escape the City meet-ups whilst planning for her big move.

She was very honest in sharing her thoughts about the process of making a big change: "Personally I've found that we're very used to our egos making the choices for us. Our egos tell us that in order to 'be' someone in the world we have to be in the right job, earn the right salary and live in the right area."

Lee told us how the hardest part of the process was breaking out and realizing that what she did and where she lived were just labels and that they would never be "who she really is". "Walking away from all that is a leap of faith and there's still a part of me that now I run a guest house wants to tell guests that I didn't always cook breakfasts and make beds, that I used to be 'important'. I have to laugh at that part of me now, the part that thought and cared about what other people thought and cared about me."

Even the most self-sufficient and independent people care what other people think about them and are subconsciously influenced by them. The Gestalt scholar and social psychology pioneer Soloman Asch recorded a famous stunt that highlighted the psychology of conformity in a 1962 Candid Camera episode called "Face The Rear". He comically highlighted the powerful influences of group pressure by getting actors to first face one direction and then another, with clueless members of the public first seeming very uncomfortable and then changing direction themselves to fit in with the crowd.

Your friends, family and other people in your life will discourage you from a decision that they perceive as being risky precisely because they care about you. They want you to have a safe, sensible job where you can afford a nice standard of living. They want to protect you from failure. You can't help but be influenced by them.

However, don't worry if you're thinking that your escape is doomed because your subconscious will always make you want to fit in with the crowd. Take some inspiration from Omar Samra's story. After almost a decade in finance he started an adventure travel company. He told us that he thinks it's up to each of us to pursue whatever story we want.

> *Some tried to talk 'sense' into me, telling me I should not go through with my plans, but perversely they just made me more stubborn and strengthened my resolve.*

Omar Samra – ex-banker, adventure company founder

We love feeling comfortable

Dave Cornthwaite (www.davecornthwaite.com) quit his job, sold his house, and has spent the last 6 years living off less than £10k a year whilst building a life around the idea of going on as many mad adventures as he can. Why? Because he realized that his life was passing him by.

This is a man who has skate-boarded across Australia, kayaked the length of the Murray River, Stand Up Paddleboarded the Mississippi River and swum down the Missouri River as part of his Expedition 1000 mission.

Dave spoke to an audience of Escape Members in London and gave us a very simple message: Comfort Kills Ambition. It's so easy to cruise through your years – achieving little, risking little – just existing.

He is on a mission to live a life worth living and, in the process, do good and inspire other people to do the same. Does this mean you should follow suit? Of course not. You may be horrified at the idea of Dave's life. However, why not take the kernel of passion and lust-for-life that is driving Dave and apply it to your own life? Why not tap into the same fear that Mr Cornthwaite has of not using his time well. If you're not doing what you want to be doing with your life perhaps you should get equally scared about the passing of time?

The fact that you're reading this book is a hint that you probably don't want to cruise comfortably through life . . . that you're looking for more. If you're anything like us you may not yet know what "more" is. Don't worry. Realizing there is an emotion that you want to act on is half the battle. The other half? Acting . . . Now that's the really hard part!

> *I studied Maths, went to university, and was comfortable in my mortgage with a steady pay cheque. However, I soon realized that I had never asked myself what I wanted out of life, what made me happy. Being happy and being comfortable are not the same thing.*
>
> **Dave Cornthwaite – adventurer**

We hate feeling scared

Rob Archer, from The Career Psychologist, recently talked to 60 Escape the City members in London about how to deal with being "headstuck". He explained how our brain's natural self-protecting mechanisms mean that we will do almost anything to avoid fear or pain in the short-term even if it is something that may massively benefit us in the longer-term. A great example of this would be turning down a public speaking invitation because of fear of embarrassment even though you know that it is a great opportunity.

He outlines four reasons why we get stuck:

1. Experiential Avoidance – this is the process of avoiding thoughts, feelings, emotions, memories and physical sensations even when doing so creates harm in the long-term. So we stay where we are, not in the service of doing something we want but in the service of avoiding difficult internal experiences. Over time this has the effect of narrowing our lives and making us stuck.

2. We are bad at making decisions – faced with a certain number of choices the human mind can get paralysed in indecision (as we outline in the next section on the paradox of choice).

3. Brains think in linear patterns – our brains like stories and we often ignore information that does not fit into our current narrative. This extends to our own careers – so what we've always done becomes all that we feel we can do.

4. We make decisions based on comparisons – we tend to make decisions based not on what we value intrinsically but on what other people value or on relative value – i.e. how our choices compare to other people.

As Rob Archer points out, if you're absolutely miserable you'll be less likely to get stuck because you'll run away from the pain (doing this has its own risks) – it's those of us who are coasting along, neither fulfilled nor absolutely miserable, who most need to beware the "headstuck" trap.

Understanding the mechanisms by which you try to avoid fear and uncertainty is a significant step towards doing something about it.

Our experience? Ultimately we decided to leave the corporate world because our frustrations outweighed our fear of making the leap. But it took us quite some time.

A big career change is scary for the same reason that the dark can be frightening. You can't see what's there and you allow your imagination to get out of control. You don't know what you don't know and you expect the worst. What the mind hates most is uncertainty.

 Dreams fade away because we can't tolerate the short-term pain necessary to get to our long-term goal.

Seth Godin – Stop Stealing Dreams

We talk ourselves out of decisions

Having no choice is obviously unbearable. However, counter-intuitively, the psychologist Barry Schwartz (who studies the links between economics and psychology) has found that freedom of choice actually makes us less happy and more dissatisfied with life. Leaving him with the conclusion, in his excellent book *The Paradox of Choice*, that the secret to happiness is low expectations.

We think that an abundance of choice is fine if you are making active choices and eliminating or pursuing new opportunities, interests and passions. As you take actions, your high expectations then become more realistic and, the more realistic they are, the more satisfied you will be with your decisions. What is important is that you actually starting making them!

You are probably familiar with the idea of Analysis Paralysis – the process of over-analysing a situation to the extent that a decision is never taken. We certainly are. Never has the theory been more applicable than to our own muddled thought processes when we were trying to escape. It's worth checking out an excellent Huffington Post article called "More Options, More Problems". It starts with "Deferring a decision means you haven't made one. Thus, some of the most talented individuals in the world find themselves stuck in an unending holding pattern . . . ".[5]

If you work in the corporate world you're probably relatively analytical. Your job might even involve analysing risk for other companies or assessing business plans. No wonder when it comes to your own life you apply the same level of rigour and risk aversion! It has become part of your thought process. A private equity analyst recently emailed us. He is desperate to start a business but has critiqued so many business plans that he is terrified of trying his own.

What good decision-making requires is for you to be clear on your decision criteria. In a career context your criteria may be anything from salary, to colleagues, to location, to creativity, to impact. Once you are clear on your criteria you can search for, eliminate and assess opportunities based on what you yourself are looking for. We'll cover this in more detail in Chapter 5 – Evolution not Revolution.

> **"** *You don't have to know what you want to do; you don't have to have it all figured out already. People in banking, in my experience, tend to be unusually risk averse, therefore before quitting (or starting) they want to be able to do some mathematical calculation of 'happiness in banking $= x + y + z$', 'happiness in something else $= A + B + C$'. They want it assured, they want the plan tight and nailed down.* **"**
>
> **Stephen Ridley, Banker turned Musician**

We are short of time and energy

An analysis of our time in the year before resigning would have shown that very little of it was spent on activities that would have led us towards a more rewarding career path. *Even though we were desperately keen to leave our jobs.*

We wanted to be exploring entrepreneurial projects and meeting new people outside of work. We were just knackered at the end of each workday. What's more, we would often spend weekends partying or distracting ourselves from the fact that we weren't enjoying our jobs. You don't have to be a life coach to spot that this behaviour wasn't helping us!

People talk about the "Eastenders Test" for assessing how committed you are to your escape. Gary Vaynerchuk calls this "The Side Hustle" in his excellently direct book *Crush It!* The logic is as follows: if you get home from a long day at work and you're prepared to spend another five hours working on your escape plan rather than watching Eastenders on TV then you're probably determined enough to make your escape a reality.

We found that we only had a limited amount of mental energy and that our job used up most of it. However, once we had focus (i.e. the idea for Escape the City) it became much easier to deprioritize everything else in favour of our escape plan. Dom managed six months of evening work building Escape the City before resigning (whilst saving up his escape fund) so he passed the test with flying colours!

> 66 *Don't go around saying that the world owes you some-thing. The world owes you nothing. It was here first.* 99
>
> **Mark Twain**

We need money to survive

You'd be amazed how many people brandish this fact at members of the Escape the City team like it was something we haven't thought about or have to confront closely ourselves.

> "But what about money?"
> "We all need money to live."
> "Oh, if I was rich of course I'd love to escape my job."

When we thought about quitting our corporate jobs we worried that we might be poor forever. We were addicted to our salaries. However, just like with the time analysis in the previous section, when we were honest with ourselves we realised that our expenditure patterns didn't reflect the life we claimed we wanted.

After taking care of our base costs we were spending all our money on distractions. Dom spent £1000 on a pair of Ralph Lauren shoes! He even bought a handmade canoe in London to train for the Yukon Canoe Race in Canada (the canoe never made it over there for the race, Dom did though). Rob bought a motorbike and spent many a weekend break in France, Spain or Italy. Mikey went on something ridiculous like six big holidays a year.

The truth is that it is very easy to get used to your salary. Your expenses rise with your income – negating any options for escape, transition, taking risks or trying something new.

Abraham Maslow's famous Hierarchy of Needs has "self-actualization" (the process of becoming your ideal self) at the top. It is at the top for an important reason. He theorized that it is impossible to fulfil our full potential if we haven't met our basic needs. So you obviously need to be in a stable position to even be able to address the question of what gives your life meaning.

Security and stability are some of the core reasons for you doing your job. However, don't be surprised if you begin to feel a nagging sense of dissatisfaction if you have stopped at those reasons. You are missing the top of the pyramid! Money isn't enough.

Worrying about money is the main reason why people stay in jobs that aren't right for them. Failing to properly deal with the financial implications of a career transition is the main reason why most escapes fail. Money is a theme that repeats through every chapter in this book (Chapter 4 is called "The Money Question" and talks you through the most sensitive and important part of your career transition).

Don't assume escaping your job has to be a blind leap of faith. Most people who successfully transition haven't allowed money fears to stop them but they most certainly have addressed their financial situation closely. You should do the same.

Take the example of Scott Gilmore; a career diplomat who was so frustrated by the inefficiencies of the aid industry and impatient to change them that he resigned from the diplomatic service on the day his first daughter was born. It sounds irresponsible. It wasn't . . .

> *The first thing I did was to talk with others who had launched their own charity or social enterprise. From them I got the sense that this would be hard, but it was possible. Then my wife and I planned our budget and decided we could afford for me to give it 6 months. If it was not making progress then I would return to government.*

Scott Gilmore – founder of Open Markets

Conclusion – Thoughts and Blockers

In this chapter we have outlined some of the forces that kept us stuck in corporate limbo for far longer than we would have liked. Gradually we realized that whilst we couldn't deny that there were forces that were keeping us where we were, they were all surmountable. Once we got our head around the fact that *we* were the main thing that was holding us back, we were able to focus on the far more exciting task of doing something about it.

There will always be reasons not to do something. Always. The reasons can seem really compelling. Often they *are* really compelling. You will feel like you're being responsible, realistic and mature. You may even explain why other people can do certain things but you can't (a very easy trap to fall into).

Ultimately, if you don't find your job fulfilling, you have to decide whether it is more responsible to keep your head down, not change, and run the risk of becoming obsolete (or worse, unhappy and bitter). Or, whether genuine responsible behaviour would see you address the blockers and begin to hunt for new opportunities.

We of all people know how hard this process is.

We also know that it is possible . . .

 Nothing will ever be attempted if all possible objections must first be overcome.

Samuel Johnson

CHAPTER 3

GRADUAL EPIPHANIES

The title of this chapter is an oxymoron. An epiphany is a sudden or striking realization – a moment of truth where everything is suddenly clear. We think that waiting for such moments can be extremely unhelpful. Rare are the moments where you "just know" what it is you want to do with your life. We believe that it is more of a process. Far more important than waiting for a sudden realization is the process of identifying the *principles* of your future life and your decision criteria.

When people talk about "Moments of Truth", they're often referring to moments where they have made a commitment to some – perhaps as yet un-defined – future action. If you're feeling stuck on The Travelator and you take anything from this book, we hope that you decide that you're going to change something without yet having to know what it is. Even if it takes you years . . . knowing that you're not going to settle is the most powerful thing you can do. It is liberating. It is exciting.

We tried not to wait for an epiphany. We began reframing the way we thought about everything. We developed our thinking and behaviour to a place where we could begin to make our choices our own. We woke up to our own values, preferences and personal truths. We shook off the shackles of our education, our parents, our friends, our colleagues and all the other well-meaning but potentially dangerous forces that had led us to where we were – stuck and unhappy.

This chapter focuses on the thoughts and gradual realisations that have worked for other people making escapes. Often all it takes to shock us out of our comfortable apathy is to read a line that strikes us as being deeply true. This chapter is split between life epiphanies and work epiphanies. We hope that the combination of the two help you overcome some of the unhelpful thoughts and blockers we explored in the previous chapter.

 Once in a while it really hits people that they don't have to experience the world in the way they have been told to. "

Alan Keightley – author

LIFE EPIPHANIES

*"You have brains in your head. You have feet in your shoes.
You can steer yourself any direction you choose.
You're on your own. And you know what you know.
And YOU are the one who'll decide where to go . . . "*

Dr. Seuss – Oh, the Places You'll Go!

Live life your way

Rob still remembers his English teacher from primary school. Mr Bradshaw was a really energetic bloke who didn't care much for rules or process. He remembers one lesson in particular when he turned to the class and said, in a conspiratorial voice . . . "Guys, you know you don't have to believe everything you learn in school? You know it's up to you what to believe?"

What a realization for a nine-year-old boy. What, so teachers and parents aren't always right?! You don't have to swallow everything whole and unquestioningly accept what you're being taught? What a great approach to life. Today Rob passionately believes that "just because" things are done in a certain way doesn't mean that that is the best way to do them and he can trace the thread of this belief all the way back to Mr Bradshaw.

Selina Barker quit her marketing job and set off to create a career that she could carry with her in a bag. Today she is an online lifestyle and career coach and she recently completed a 6-month adventure living and working from a camper van, travelling around the UK.

She told us that she knew she didn't want a life of 9–5 routine; stuck in an office, working for someone else: "All I ever seemed to get back from people was 'well, I'm afraid you just have to, that's just how things are'. It was like a red rag to a bull – there's nothing that motivates me more than being told something isn't possible."

Omar Samra, the investment banker who started Wild Guanabana, the adventure and travel company, said that he had a moment of truth when climbing a mountain in West Papua: "What was I doing wasting my life living someone else's? I returned home and within a week I had resigned."

A nurse called Bronnie Ware recorded the top regrets of people in their last days of life. She wrote about the clarity people have at the end of their lives and how we can learn from their wisdom. The same themes repeated. The number one regret was "I wish I'd had the courage to live a life true to myself, not the life others expected of me."[1]

Our take? You have to live the life YOU want, not the life that someone else wants for you – especially if it's easier not to.

To be nobody but yourself – in a world which is doing its best, night and day, to make you everybody else – means to fight the hardest battle which any human being can fight; and never stop fighting.

e. e cummings

Heed the call

Adam Fenton used to work in IT at an investment bank. He wasn't happy. He had been carried along by the perceived prestige of working for his employer but the recession made his job even more stressful and unfulfilling. He went through many of the now familiar thoughts about what he could and couldn't do: "what will my parents/family/friends think?" and "am I giving up the chance to advance in a great career?"

Then he started to look at the risk of not quitting his job and following his dream. The possibility that he would regret not taking a decision in a few years helped him make up his mind and he resigned: "On March 17th 2011 I jumped on a flight to Sao Paulo with a backpack in the hold and a one-way ticket in my hand. And not for one second have I regretted that decision nor missed my desk in London. It was the best decision of my life!"

Since he started travelling and working from the road, Adam has lived in Colombia, travelled around South America and has now fallen in love with Mexico. He told us: ". . . just go with whatever feels right at the time and stay confident that things will work out. And try re-framing the risks you perceive in following your heart – for example, what are the risks of NOT doing so?"

Ideas come and go. They aren't all worth quitting your job for. However, once the kernel of an idea that excites you has implanted itself in your mind you might find that it keeps coming back again and again. Once we had discussed the idea for Escape the City (and Dom had designed the little Escape key mascot) we found we just couldn't stop thinking about it. The sure-fire sign that we were going to have to act on the idea was that we were far, far more excited about it than our jobs. We didn't want to regret trying and we were prepared to put ourselves in a position where we might fail for a shot at it.

> *There you are, minding your own business, then suddenly you feel 'The Call'. The call to do something totally insane and futile. But you know you have to do it. You know that if you don't, a little part of you will be dead forever.*
>
> **Hugh Macleod – thegapingvoid.com**

Avoid living for the future

Living for the future.

Tim Ferriss (author of *The 4-Hour Work Week*) calls it The Deferred Life Plan. Alastair Humphreys (who cycled around the world) calls it The Race To The Biggest Gravestone. Randy Komisar (author of *The Monk and The Riddle*) calls it "The Biggest Risk of All" (the risk of spending your life not doing what you want on the bet you can buy yourself the freedom to do it later). In the context of corporate jobs, we call it the "I'll Do This For 5 Years And Then I'll Go Do Something Else" promise.

Our moment of truth came when we realized that we were no longer kids and that it was time to take responsibility for our path in life. Just the other day we were fresh-faced graduates with ideals, naïvety and dreams. Then suddenly we were getting grey hairs. Time started going by really fast and, for some reason (perhaps it was the routine of the corporate world) seemed to be accelerating! Why were we spending our precious time doing things that didn't matter to us?!

Spending time doing work that you don't want to do, you are wasting valuable time that could be spent discovering new interests and developing skills, contacts and experiences in new areas.

 It's the oldest story in the world. One day you're 17 and you're planning for someday. And then quietly, without your ever really noticing, someday is today. And then someday is yesterday. And this is your life.

Nathan Scott – One Tree Hill[2]

𝚎𝚜𝚌 **Realize nothing stays the same**

Our lives are relatively short. The arc of human history is much longer than any single lifetime. It is easy to fall into the trap of believing that things have always been the way they are. However, "that's just the way things are" is a rubbish excuse for inaction – if you can be sure of one thing it's that things will not be like this for long.

The story of human civilization so far has been one of constant change. Let's not fall into the trap of patronizing future generations by thinking that today's world – with all its amazing achievements and stunning failures – is the end of progress, change or human evolution. If anything, the pace of change is accelerating.[3]

In most developed countries life expectancy is rising. A recent study suggests that half of babies born in the UK in 2000 will live beyond their 100th birthday.[4] The paradigms of the 20th century will change (they must change) to adapt to a new way of living in the 21st century. Retire at 65? No thanks, I'm only just getting going. Work for 40 years in one physical location for one single organization? What a quaint idea!

Ten years ago it would have been amazing to consider having your music, your camera, your phone and your watch in one device. Today the smart phone in your pocket provides you with access to huge amounts of information. Your parents might have spent a year in the library to find what you can find via Google in a few hours of intelligent searching. In a world where information is immediately available a good education becomes less about memorizing facts and more about teaching people how to search for, process and assess information.

We recently met with Mark Stevenson, author of *The Optimist's Tour of the Future*, who shared his opinion that the way in which technology is changing how we live, how we communicate and how we conduct business is just the *hors d'oeuvre* for far greater changes to come (and they're coming soon).

The problem with the Travelator mentality is that it encourages you to identify a box, plant yourself squarely in that box, and keep your head down until you retire. Behaving like this used to be a safe way of managing your career (unless a recession took your job) because organizations wanted people who could run processes and conform to spec. Today this approach guarantees obsolescence. What we need more than ever is ways to ensure our continuing relevance.

You need to understand the changes that your job title, skill set, employer and industry are facing. This is a crucial element of being able to benefit from new opportunities. Over the coming pages we will look at some specific ways of exposing yourself to new ideas, information and people in order to better grasp the opportunities of the future.

 It is not the strongest of species that survive, nor the most intelligent, but the ones most responsive to change.

Charles Darwin

Preempt the big scare or tragedy

Lea Woodward runs three different online businesses, including LocationIndependent.com. In 2003 she was a management consultant working at Accenture when her mother unexpectedly and extremely sadly passed away after a complication during her fight with cancer. After two weeks of compassionate leave she was back on the job.

She recently shared her career transition with a room full of Escape the City members on the ninth anniversary of her mum's death. It was extremely emotional to hear her talk about how the experience shocked her into realising that she needed to do something different.

"I couldn't go back to what I knew and so I took a sabbatical which then just reaffirmed what I'd been feeling for a long time. I'd never planned to stay in consulting for so long but became stuck in the 'not knowing what else to do' and earning lots of money traps. As soon as I had some breathing space from the daily grind, it was obvious that I needed to do something else."

So many people make big life changes just after experiencing a personal tragedy or a near tragedy. If you have already experienced something similar, you will know what we mean. It can shake everything into focus and simplify life down to the few things that really matter.

It is too easy for dissatisfaction to be dormant for a long time. What does it say about our ability to endure situations that make us unhappy that it requires something really sad to shock us out of our complacency? Don't wait for something awful to happen to spur you to change.

> ❝ It seems that most of us could benefit from a brush with a near-fatal disaster to help us recognise the important things that we are too defeated or embittered to recognise from day to day. ❞
>
> **Alain de Botton – A Week at the Airport: A Heathrow Diary**

Write your own obituary

Meet Roz Savage.

The year is 2000. She is 33 years old. She seems to have the perfect life: a job (management consultant, of course!), a husband, a home and a little red sports car. Fast forward to March 2006, she is 38, divorced, homeless, and alone in a tiny rowing boat in the middle of the Atlantic Ocean. Today she is a world-famous, TED-speaking adventurer and environmental campaigner.[5]

How did this happen? One day, fed up with sitting on the commuter train "wondering whether this was what life was all about", she sat down and wrote two versions of her obituary. The first one was the one she wanted to have. The second one was the one that she was heading for. In her own words: "the difference between the two was startling. Clearly something was going to have to change."

We're not suggesting that you should quit your job and go and row around the world. The thoughts that drove Roz to make such big changes and the subsequent process of transitioning are what make this story relevant. It is easy to get so bound up in the race to climb your career ladder that you can often forget to ask whether you are climbing the right one. Looking ahead to the end of your life can be a powerful way of putting your week-to-week decisions and worries in perspective.

> **❝** *If you were to die right now, how would you feel about your life?* **❞**
>
> **Tyler Durden – Fight Club[6]**

Avoid empty "find yourself" advice

Traditional career advice tells us that in order to know why you aren't enjoying your job you need to understand who you really are. Rob Archer, from The Career Psychologist, thinks that trying to discover yourself (or at least your true "self") is dangerous advice. Speaking at a recent Esc event he reminded us that humans are not types, he quoted the last line of Walt Whitman's poem *Songs of Myself*: "I am large, I contain multitudes." Beware psychometric tests!

He says that thinking of yourself as a type or as having a true "self" is as likely to get you stuck as set you free because humans don't have true selves. We create ourselves. He says that there are many aspects of who you are. You contain many potential selves. What matters more is the kind of "you" you want to create. You are not one thing, he says, you need to realize that you can construct yourself.

A recent commenter on the Escape the City blog told us that "so many of us forget what happiness is really like". She then explained how the urgency of keeping up with the treadmill of conventional life often means that people forget not "who they are" but "what they enjoy".

In an article called "It's Not About You" in the *New York Times*,[7] David Brooks explains that "most successful [. . .] people don't look inside and then plan a life. They look outside and find a problem, which summons their life. [Most people] are called by a problem, and the self is constructed gradually by their calling."

Our decision to escape the corporate world wasn't so much a sudden realization of "who we were" but a gradual remembering of the things that we enjoyed contrasted with the things that we didn't. The years we spent in that environment were invaluable because they showed us the importance of spending the rest of our careers striving to do things that mattered to us.

Of course you need to make career decisions based on a proper understanding of your values. Failing to do so means you can easily end up in another job that isn't right for you. However, it does seem that following "your passion" based on "your true self" is a trap worth avoiding as it could just as easily lead you to anti-climax as liberate you.

  Life isn't about finding yourself. Life is about creating yourself.

George Bernard Shaw

WORK EPIPHANIES

"I didn't want 'Grumpy Investment Banker' on my tombstone."

Rob Owen – ex-finance professional now CEO at St. Giles Trust – a charity that helps break the cycle of offending

`esc` **Recognize the signs**

Alastair Humphreys (www.alastairhumphreys.com), who makes a living as an adventurer, author and speaker, recently wrote an excellent article called "20 Questions Worth Answering Honestly".[8]

Here are the first five:

1. Do you earn enough money?

2. Do you enjoy your job?

3. Do you prefer Saturday or Monday?

4. What would you like to be doing one year from now?

5. What would you like to be doing five years from now?

When we answered these questions, we realized that we were wishing away our lives, simply living for the next holiday or weekend. All three of us have stories that indicated that we were doing ourselves more harm than good by delaying the decision to leave.

The problem was that we were coasting. It was really easy to get by for quite a while without exerting ourselves and without being so unhappy that we simply had to leave. If you genuinely hate your job and couldn't stand a single minute more at work you would probably leave no matter the cost.

Dr Sherry Moss is an Associate Professor of Organizational Studies at a business school in the USA. She teaches MBA students and spends a lot of time wondering about the working world she is preparing people for. She recently suggested that there are 19 different sources of meaning to be found in work (shown on the next page).

Reflecting back on our corporate jobs we can only recognize 9, 10, 15 and 16 as significant sources of meaning. Once we accepted that these weren't enough we knew we had to get out of there.

Which sources of meaning does your job provide you with?
Which do you want your job to provide you with?

19 different sources of meaning in work:

1. Seeing a tangible outcome from one's work
2. Status/prestige
3. Importance to society
4. A sense of calling
5. Helping others
6. Total identification with the organization and its mission
7. Work as a source of fun/energy
8. Complete belief in the product/service one represents
9. Work to support family
10. Work as a sense of duty/obligation
11. Work as basic human dignity
12. Challenge and accomplishment
13. Winning
14. Developing others
15. Instrumental – work now to play later
16. Work with the pure goal of making money and becoming rich
17. To set a good example for one's children
18. For independence, control or autonomy
19. To have meaningful relationships with co-workers or others with whom one works

"Why We Work: Finding Meaning in Your Job", by Dr Sherry Moss in *HuffingtonPost.com*[9]

Stop collecting qualifications

Qualifications are important for certain career paths. For example, if you've decided you want to transition into an area that requires a specific degree. They are often a great form of external validation: "Oh that person must be smart/capable, they studied at XXXX. . . . "

However, all too often further education is a massive form of procrastination. We know this because we were extremely tempted to enrol on MBAs as a way to take some time out from work without it feeling unconstructive. Rob even considered doing a winemaking masters in Australia (the fact that he wasn't qualified to get onto the course and couldn't afford it seemed to have escaped him).

The problem with further study as a form of delaying the hard work of figuring out what you want to do next is that it often compounds the situation. You qualify with even more debt and if you elevate your salary expectations with your new qualification you can limit your choices right down to the biggest (and sometimes the most boring) companies in the world.

There are times when there is a clear case for learning an additional skill or getting another degree. To open a new door, to make you eligible for a job that you know you already want to do. However, a lot of the time the additional qualification is undertaken as a way of avoiding the decision of what to do next.

Focusing on collecting qualifications can be to the detriment of real-life experience. OK, so you can study and pass exams what have you ever done in the real world? Can you deliver projects, execute plans and get stuff done?

If you work your way down the Forbes 400 making an x next to the name of each person with an MBA, you'll learn something important about business school. After Warren Buffett, you don't hit another MBA till number 22, Phil Knight, the CEO of Nike. There are only 5 MBAs in the top 50.

Paul Graham – founder of tech incubator "Y Combinator"

Look up the ladder

Stephen Ridley escaped investment banking to be a musician: 24 hours after quitting his job, he rolled an upright piano into the middle of one of London's busiest streets and started playing. After 1 month he had been offered 9 management deals, and started recording his first album, "Butterfly In A Hurricane", now on iTunes. He recently played an amazing live set at Escape the City's third birthday party in London.

The moment he realized there was no one more senior than him in the bank whom he aspired to be like was the moment he knew he had to get out: "I looked above me and I didn't see these sharp, shiny, successful men that I imagined I'd one day become by working at an investment bank. No. I saw uninspired, bland, middle-aged men, drearily pushing their crushed souls through another long day of the same old slog."

Our thought processes were similar to Stephen's. We decided to escape when we realized that we didn't want our boss's job or their boss's job. It wasn't that we weren't prepared to work hard and pay our dues from our relatively junior positions; it was that we didn't think the sacrifices were worth the eventual end goal.

Once you realize that there is no one higher up than you whose job you want it should then become a question of "when do I leave?" not "if".

Furthermore, remember that most of you are expected to leave at some point. Big corporates operate on a pyramid structure. There are a lot more people at the bottom than at the top. It may be stating the obvious but if you don't properly enjoy the work then you're probably not going to have the grit and determination it takes to climb the ladder in any case.

It wasn't a particularly long stint in the City – but it was long enough for me to realize that I didn't enjoy the culture, the working conditions (the trading floor is actually scarily similar to battery hen farming!) and the politics. And most of all, I never found a boss to whom I could look up to and aspire to be.

Caroline Dean – ex-banker turned entrepreneur

Accept changing is always hard

It is counter-intuitive, especially as our culture has such a stigma around quitting, but sometimes it is much harder to decide to call something a day than to carry on.

Seth Godin has written an excellent little book on this called *The Dip – A Little Book That Teaches You When to Quit (and When to Stick)*. In it he prompts you to identify Dips (which might get better if you keep pushing) versus Cul-de-Sacs (which won't get better no matter how hard you try). Winners, he says, are better than the rest of us at spotting the difference. Winners "quit fast, quit often and quit without guilt", until they commit to beating the right dip for the right reasons.

We decided to quit when we realized that if we didn't want to work in our industries long-term, then five years extra experience wasn't going to help and could even harm our careers. It was hard to fight our natural "loss aversion" (the idea that the more you invest time and effort into something, the less you can view its success or failure objectively and the harder it is to decide to change).

Louisa Blackmore escaped from the heart of the CITY where she worked for a hedge fund (and before that a magic circle law firm). She quit to launch her own interior design company. She was on a flight to the USA for her cousin's wedding. When she turned off her BlackBerry she realized she was the happiest she'd been in months. She had harboured the idea for her company, West Egg, for over two years but never thought she would have the guts to actually quit her job and start it . . .

> **❝** *Then it suddenly dawned on me, if I didn't do it now I probably never would and that terrified me more than the thought of failing.* **❞**
>
> **Louisa Blackmore – ex-corporate professional, entrepreneur**

Choose a fight worth fighting

We've already mentioned Scott Gilmore, the career diplomat, who was so frustrated by the inefficiencies of the aid industry that he quit to launch a social enterprise called Open Markets. It is on a mission to build markets and create jobs in developing countries. They now have 150 staff working around the world and have created over 77,000 jobs in some the world's poorest places.

Many of us working in the corporate world, even if we don't necessarily work for the "bad guys", often have an uncomfortable feeling that our values aren't aligned with those of our employer. This is one of the most important ingredients in job satisfaction. It is much easier to work hard and make sacrifices for an organization when you agree with the overall vision.

You don't have to do work that saves the world but you do have a responsibility to have a positive impact in some form through your work. Besides, returning to more selfish motives, working on something you believe in is the surest way to fulfilling work.

There are so many fights worth fighting.

Are you part of the problem or part of the solution?

> " *In the new world of work, the purpose of work is not just to contribute your skills to a company or industry and in exchange make enough money to take care of yourself and your family. Rather, the purpose of work is to allow you to create and contribute a meaningful, useful, and beautiful body of work to the world and along the way, take care of your financial needs. To do this, you need a new framework, new skills and a new approach to your entire work life.* "
>
> **Pamela Slim** – Escape from Cubicle Nation

Decide that enough is enough

David Attenborough started his career in publishing. He decided to escape when time seemed to be passing so slowly that he thought that the clock he could see from his desk on London's St Paul's cathedral was broken. He was fortunate enough to have his moment of truth aged 24. I doubt anyone who is familiar with his life's work or has read his book *Life On Air* would say that he made the wrong decision.

Conventional wisdom would have told him to stay in his job for at least two years (for the CV) and to weigh up his options carefully before deciding which career path to take. Conventional wisdom would have been wrong.

We read his book when we were having our own little career crises and wondering what to do with our lives. We used to meet on the steps of St Paul's cathedral to discuss our escape plans. We were within yards of where Attenborough had had his realization back in the 1950s. His story struck us because we were in exactly the same situation as him, wondering whether we had really studied for three years to get our degree to find ourselves sitting in an office, clock-watching, and doing work that didn't interest us.

How will you know when enough is enough? Perhaps you never will. Perhaps you'll be there forever. Or perhaps you've already had an inkling that there is more to life and are taking the small steps towards finding out what it is that you actually want to spend your time doing . . .

> 66
>
> *The clock hadn't stopped after all. Its hands had certainly moved. They had advanced a few minutes [. . .] I decided to turn my desk around so that I wasn't hypnotised by the hands of a clock. And it was then that I decided that this was not the way I wanted to spend the rest of my life. . . .*
>
> 99
>
> **David Attenborough – Life on Air**

Conclusion – Gradual Epiphanies

Our gradual epiphanies came once we assessed the benefits of our jobs against the sacrifices. By being honest about the reality of our situation we realized that every moment we stayed there was a moment that we weren't building the futures we wanted for ourselves. Our most important realization was that there would never be a perfect time to do something that felt scary or risky.

We didn't want to be known as those people that hated their jobs but did nothing about it. We didn't have to make the decision to quit to start exploring new opportunities. We were simply making a decision *to try and get ourselves in a position* where we could make a proper decision. We were inching our way towards the end of the plank.

You don't have to have "found your calling" in order to do stuff that you enjoy. Once you take away the pressure of asking "is this what I really want to do with my life?" you make it much easier to take on new ideas, opportunities and challenges. If you give yourself a break for not having it all figured out yet the world can seem like a much more exciting place.

You can resolve to make a big career change before knowing what you are escaping towards. However, you can't just run away from something, you also need to run towards something. So, whilst you figure this one out, start saving! The next chapter deals with that crucial issue – money – before we go on to explore how any escape should involve evolution not revolution in the chapter on transitioning.

> **❝** *I saw that my life was a vast glowing empty page and I could do anything I wanted.* **❞**
>
> **Jack Kerouac**

CHAPTER 4
THE MONEY QUESTION

The main reason people stay in jobs they don't enjoy is money. This is a pretty good reason. When you have debts to pay, mortgages to service and a whole variety of other monthly outgoings it is hard to consider taking any form of career risk at all. When you are planning an escape or career transition, you will think about the money question A LOT. It will be one of your main decision criteria. If you're determined to make an escape then don't let it become one of your mental blockers.

Here are some common thoughts . . .

- "I don't have lots of savings so I can't risk escaping."

- "I can't possibly ever earn less than what I earn today."

If building a fulfilling career on your own terms AND earning pots of cash were easy then everyone would be doing it. There is an amount of money that everyone needs to afford a certain standard of living. Above that it is down to your values and preferences (once you have covered your "needs" it comes down to your "wants"). There is no value judgement here. You may equate security and success with a certain amount of money in the bank. That's fine. This is not a rant on the evils of money. It comes down to the question of "what do you want?" As long as it is stuff that you genuinely know you want (rather than ideas you have inherited from other peoples' value systems) then great . . . pursue it . . . it's what you want.

Your costs will increase as you get older. And they don't increase incrementally. They increase in jumps. BUYING A HOUSE – big jump. GETTING MARRIED – big jump. HAVING KIDS – massive jump! This means two things: 1) every year that you leave it before you make a big career change is likely a year closer to your next jump, 2) even if you have no particular "responsibilities" today you already have one eye on the next jump. So it's not as simple as saying "you're free today" . . . "act as if you'll always be free!"

You're a responsible person (and probably more conservative than you realize) and you're planning for the future. Is it possible to plan for the future and live a life of your choosing in the present? This is not a choice between being poor and happy or rich and unhappy. Any corporate escape has to be viable otherwise it won't last. Don't fall into the trap of thinking you have to sacrifice financial security for a life of meaning.

Whatever your escape, you need to do the sums between what finances you've got at your disposal for the transition and what amount of money you *want* (not just need) to have to feel secure through this time. Then you can make a personal judgement regarding the levels of risk you're willing to face.

Through this chapter we refer to "The Hit". This is the number of months' worth of living costs you need to cover between turning off your salary and the eventual thing you are escaping to (your new job or business once it is established). The number you are aiming at is the amount you need to bridge this period – your Escape Fund. We expand on these ideas in the following pages.

"The Money Question" deserves a book in itself. This chapter contains some prompts for thinking about money differently as well as practical advice for how to manage your finances in the context of an escape plan.

There are, of course, trade-offs (especially in the short-term), which we'll discuss. The main traits required for a successful answer to the money question are planning and discipline. Manage the money question and you will be successfully addressing the biggest reason why most escapes fail.

> *Too many people spend money they haven't earned, to buy things they don't want, to impress people they don't like.*
>
> **Will Rogers – cowboy, vaudeville performer, humourist**

THINK ABOUT YOUR FINANCES DIFFERENTLY

"Busy yourself with the routine of the money wheel, pretend it's the fix-all, and you artfully create a constant distraction that prevents you from seeing just how pointless it is. Deep down, you know it's all an illusion, but with everyone participating in the same game of make-believe, it's easy to forget. The problem is more than money."

Tim Ferriss **– The 4-Hour Work Week**

The golden handcuffs

Having more money should lead to greater freedom but paradoxically often leads to greater entrapment. Broadly speaking, the more money we have, the more options we have. Money can allow us to take risks, explore new opportunities, start businesses, fund projects or retrain in other sectors. However, all too often unfortunately, money seems to trap us. This is what Rousseau meant when he said "the money you have can give you freedom; the money you pursue enslaves you".

If you are anything like us, your expenses will keep track with your income. The more we earned the more we spent. In doing so, we were getting ourselves further and further away from a place where we had flexibility and options. The golden handcuffs are real – both in terms of your expenses rising with your income and the mental barriers that you develop against ever earning less than your current salary.

We spent a lot of time in and around our jobs spending our salaries distracting ourselves from the growing sense of emptiness and dissatisfaction that our jobs were giving us. The higher our salaries rose, the more we were able to spend (rather than save!) and the more we went into debt. Money is an enabler – it should allow you to do things you want to do rather than being an end in itself. It's up to you to decide what you want it to enable you to do. Save and you buy yourself options. Spend and you can become trapped.

 Money is multiplied in practical value depending on the number of W's you control in your life: what you do, when you do it, where you do it, and with whom you do it. I call this the freedom multiplier.

Timothy Ferriss – The 4-Hour Work Week

esc Money and happiness

Being poor is no one's idea of fun. So, how much money buys happiness? *Does* money buy happiness??

Research suggests the "happiness" number is approximately forty thousand dollars a year in the USA. Daniel Gilbert is a professor of psychology at Harvard University who delivered a TED talk on "The surprising science of happiness".[1] He claims that once you have enough money to meet your basic needs (food, shelter, but not necessarily satellite TV) incremental increases have little effect on your happiness.

Richard Easterlin, professor of economics at the University of Southern California, says that our desires adjust to our income. "At all levels of income, the typical response is that one needs 20% more to be happy." Once you have basic needs covered (which is going to be a different financial threshold depending where you live), the generalization seems to be true – increasing your wealth alone does not increase your happiness.

In *Would You Be Happier If You Were Richer?*,[2] Daniel Kahneman, Nobel prize-winning psychologist, suggests there has to be more than a salary for you to really care about your job. It's not that wealth is bad. It's that the single-minded pursuit of wealth above other values leads many people to feel rather empty. The lesson is clear – "don't worship money".

Obviously it is impossible to be happy and professionally fulfilled if you can't take care of your basic needs at the bottom of Maslow's pyramid. However, it seems that having enough money to meet all your needs and more does not make you happy by itself. You probably already know this. However, does your career behaviour reflect that knowledge?

When we worked in the corporate world we had more money than we ever had before. When we worked as bootstrapping entrepreneurs we had even less money than we did at university. We have found that working on something that really matters to you can outweigh not having as much money as you did previously.

You have to choose a process that you enjoy (building a business that you love, finding a job that makes you tick) because the end goal (wealth, retirement, power, status, massive house) – if you ever reach it – is so often an anti-climax.

We have been brought up in a society surrounded by people striving for more – more money, more possessions, more status and more power. This 'size-matters' attitude reminds us of Seth Godin's quote: "Bigger doesn't equal better, better equals better."

How much is enough?
How much is enough for you?

 Nearly every financial situation reflects one of three general patterns: seeing oneself as having less than enough, just enough, or more than enough money. The term 'enough' is relative and highly individualized. For some people, having basic needs met is sufficient, engendering a sense of satisfaction and security; among others, no matter how much money they accumulate, the perception persists that they need more.

Pamela Slim – Escape from Cubicle Nation

esc The cycle of consumption

A common criticism of today's developed world is that we are all addicted to buying things. The anti-consumerist argument is that we are being conditioned by hundreds of advertising messages to meet our emotional needs through consumption and, as a result, we are less happy (or certainly no happier). We under-appreciate truly valuable things in pursuit of more money in order to buy more stuff. Firstly, is this a fair analysis? And, secondly, why is this relevant if you want to escape your job?

Let's return briefly to the question of happiness. David Myers (another psychologist!) calculated that although the real, inflation-adjusted income of Americans doubled between 1960 and 1990, the proportion of Americans describing themselves as "very happy" remained at 30%.[3] Psychologists call the phenomenon of chasing after rewards that don't provide lasting satisfaction the "hedonic treadmill". Now we're not complaining about being materially better off, but what is going on if this hasn't been matched by corresponding increases in emotional and mental wellbeing?

It turns out that the chemical dopamine might provide some explanation.[4] Dopamine is a core part of the brain's reward mechanism and, as a result, a key component in our consumerist desires. When something "good" happens (we get a new job, we read a nice email, or we buy some new shoes) dopamine is secreted in our brains. This makes us feel good. The brain associates this good feeling with the behaviour, which in turn reinforces the initial activity (be it shopping, checking email or having sex). Habits (good and bad) form in this way.

Peter Whybrow, head of the Semel Institute for Neuroscience and Behavior at UCLA, has written a book called *American Mania: When More Is Not Enough*. In it he defends dopamine as being an extremely important reason why humans have survived and prospered. "We're primed for doing things immediately", he tells us, "We're poor at planning for the future". The drive for instant gratification was evolutionarily extremely useful when trying to survive from day to day in the savannah 10,000 years ago. However, it seems it is slightly less helpful in today's developed-country environment where we are already surrounded by abundance.

University of Michigan professor of psychology Kent Berridge has proposed that the brain can become sensitized to the cycle of desire behind a particular reward.[5] So we become increasingly driven to a particular behaviour at the same time as the reward becomes less rewarding. This basic overview of brain chemistry goes some way to explaining why our short-term desires can be so powerful, why addictions are so hard to beat and why we can never get enough of buying stuff.

The economist Victor Lebow stated how "our enormously productive economy demands that we make consumption our way of life, that we convert the buying and use of goods into rituals, that we seek our spiritual satisfaction and our ego satisfaction in consumption".[6] And he said that in 1955!

You don't have to be a psychologist to realize that excessive focus on money and consumption might not be great for our mental health. A large survey of randomly selected adults, sponsored by the National Institute of Mental Health (NIMH) and conducted between 2001 and 2003, found that an astonishing 46% met criteria established by the American Psychiatric Association (APA) for having had at least one mental illness within four broad categories at some time in their lives.[7]

The controversial Kalle Lasn, founder of AdBusters, has some strong views on the links between advertising and mental illness, citing a study by Myra Whiteman at Columbia University and one by the World Health Organization: "Young people are 300% more likely to suffer from depression, or mood disorders, or panic attacks than my generation. There's been a terrible degradation of our mental environment [. . .] People are making this connection between their stress levels [. . .] and the ads. . . . "[8]

It is a compelling, if depressing, narrative and one that we lived ourselves. As we have mentioned, this is particularly relevant within the context of career dissatisfaction. Our own experiences of over-spending in order to alleviate job unhappiness (before we decided to start saving) delayed our escapes by at least 12 months.

The quick fix for feeling miserable is often to spend money on yourself (ironically making you even more dependent on the job that is making you unhappy). Now of course money isn't bad, of course shopping isn't evil. Don't look for blanket extremism where there is none. However, the more aware we can be of our own behaviour and the more we can understand how our minds work, the more we can actively decide what we spend our money on. Just as spending money on worthless or short-term gratification is unsatisfying, spending money on things of genuine value can lead to a much more rewarding existence.

Wants and needs. Do you need all the things you think you need? And, once you really challenge yourself, do you even truly *want* them either? And finally (if you're feeling a little overwhelmed) why not watch George Carlin's sketch about "Stuff" for some light-hearted relief! http://www.youtube.com/watch?v=MvgN5gCuLac.

 The human race has had long experience and a fine tradition in surviving adversity. But we now face a task for which we have little experience, the task of surviving prosperity.

Alan Gregg – Canadian political advisor

Escape begins with definition

Charles Givens, the American personal finance guru, gives this advice in *Wealth Without Risk*: "Ask yourself: 'If I had unlimited, time, talent, money, ability, self-confidence and support from my family, what would I do?' Then, list the steps necessary to achieve these goals."

OK, so you don't have unlimited time and money . . . but what he wants you to do is envision goals beyond the constraints of your current situation. This is hard but not impossible. It's amazing what can be achieved by breaking big objectives into step-by-step activities.

One of the first things you should do when planning a career escape is define your needs and wants. What is your 100% non-negotiable minimum annual income? Or not even minimum . . . what is the figure you want to be earning after you've successfully escaped?

Realize that there may be a period of transition when you don't earn this amount ("the Hit"). It's up to you how long this period is. Just as it is up to you to reject situations where the period is longer than you are prepared to accept or can afford. This is a very personal and subjective part of your career transition.

If escape begins with definition you need to be clear on two things:

1. That you know how much money you need for the life you want.

2. That you have been really honest that this genuinely is the life you want (and not the life that you think you want).

Money has no value without context. In the bank it may provide you with a feeling of security. But the pre-requisite is that you value that feeling of security . . . otherwise it is just a number. In order to have congruence between your financial goals and your objectives in life, you need to set goals for what your money will ENABLE you to do.

Therefore it can't just be a number, it should be a number plus an objective (it could be a house, it could be private school for your kids, or it could be owning a hotel on the beach in Africa). The objective is entirely up to you – just make sure it is yours and no one else's.

66 *Money itself isn't the primary factor in what one does. A person does things for the sake of accomplishing something. Money generally follows.* 99

Colonel Henry Crown – industrialist, philanthropist

Redefine personal finance

Soul Patel (www.soulpatel.com) is a successful corporate escapee who is building an independent property portfolio (yes, without being rich in the first place). He is also a personal finance expert. He recently ran a workshop for Escape the City members where he talked about how your salary is your most valuable asset. Consistent, recurring, predictable income is hugely valuable when planning an escape.

The key idea was that if something is not paying you a return then it should be defined as a liability, not an asset. Why? If you lose your job these liabilities will continue to take more and more money from you until you are bankrupt. So your house, your car – these are all liabilities, often mistaken for assets. Examples of assets include shares, bonds, investment properties and businesses, however education and skill is needed to manage these, otherwise they can become liabilities too.

If you're reading this from the security of a decently paid corporate job, know this: you have one great advantage at the moment – yes, your job! At our event Soul reminded the room how the main thing a job provides you with is cash flow. He told us how most people squander this and he challenged us about getting trapped in the cycle of consumption, by allowing our expenses to stay high, taking on debt, and by investing our money in liabilities thinking they are assets.

> **66** *We go to school to learn to work hard for money. I [...] teach people how to have money work hard for them.* **99**
>
> **Robert Kiyosaki – Rich Dad, Poor Dad**

MANAGE YOUR FINANCES DIFFERENTLY

*"Money frees you from doing things you dislike.
Since I dislike doing nearly everything, money is handy."*

Groucho Marx

esc Conduct a personal financial audit

Before you even consider quitting your job you need to get a clear picture of your current situation. It's not good enough to just add up what you have in the bank. You need to have a clear picture of the following four numbers:

- Income (revenue)

- Expenses (costs)

- Investments (assets)

- Debt (liabilities)

Pamela Slim has written an excellent guide to managing your personal finances around an escape (for her readers it is within the context of escaping to build a business). She gives the following advice:

> *Let your fears guide you: Fears are not all bad! They can be a great way to ensure that your plan covers what it needs to. If you have a nagging fear about something that is not covered in your current plan, it is a good indication that you need to address it.*
>
> *– How will I pay for a medical emergency?*
> *– How will I replace paid time off?*
> *– How much am I really going to pay in taxes?*
> *– What if my clients don't pay on time?*
> *– What if I get sued by a client or competitor?*
>
> **Pamela Slim – Escape from Cubicle Nation**

Crunch the numbers behind your escape

Getting your head around The Money Question is a process of clarifying your goals, your levels of risk tolerance and four key numbers:

A. The minimum you can live on per month (during your escape).

B. How many months you think you'll need to live on it for (the Hit).

C. Your ideal recurring income after the transition (post-escape).

D. Your total escape fund (your pre-escape savings).

The magic number is D – your target saving amount – and the minimum acceptable amount to resign on is A x B (i.e. the amount you need per month multiplied by the number of months you think your transition will take). Then you tell yourself that after "B" months you need to be at "C" otherwise you'll rethink your plans or go back to your old job. NB: You may have a part-time work plan for the transition. This can further extend the period you have to make your escape work.

You may be in a fortunate situation whereby you can forecast every number without doubt. However, if your escape involves the prospect of an as-yet-unknown income stream (a new salary or a sustainable business venture) then the anticipated date of that money (C) hitting your bank account is the big risk in the calculation and it is probably worth inflating (B) by at least 25% as insurance.

If you are serious about escaping then the easiest deadline to set yourself for resignation is the day that you hit your magic number – D – the number that you need to cover you through the Hit. This gives you something to aim at and helps with the discipline of saving. It also takes away the fear of wondering when the right time is to quit (hint: there is no right time, so you might as well make it the day you hit your magic number!).

To state the obvious, personal finance is personal. Just as you shouldn't let anyone else determine your goals and values, you should also seek to maintain control over your own financial priorities. More than almost any other aspect of identity, if you don't have clarity of purpose over how you view the role of money in your life, you'll likely end up going along with what other people do.

Chris Guillebeau – The Art of Non-Conformity

See your escape as a startup

Every business has revenues and costs, assets and liabilities. Your personal finances are no different. Every startup has to get their revenues above their costs before they run out of time (and money). Your escape is the same (whether or not you're building a business).

You have revenue streams (your salary and any other incomings). You have costs (your rent, your living expenses, etc). If your revenues are above your costs no one can stop you. You can move both numbers. Seen in this light, your job is just a revenue stream that you are particularly emotionally attached to.

Startups have a certain amount of time to find a scalable business model before they go bust. You are a person in search of a scalable new career. You have a certain amount of time to figure out your "business model" before you go bust (i.e. before you have to go back to your old job or find a new job).

Just like a startup you should do a few key things:

1. Keep your costs as low as possible whilst you're finding the way that works.

2. Get someone to pay you for something (anything) whilst you figure things out.

3. Know what your monthly burn-rate is (therefore know how many "months-till-death" you have).

4. Place small bets and test towards the way that works (rather than guessing or planning your way through uncertainty).

> 66 *A startup is an organization formed to search for a repeatable and scalable business model.* 99
>
> **Steve Blank – www.steveblank.com**

esc Minimise costs

Dom wrote a fantastic escape diary tracing his thoughts and fears as he worked his final three months in the corporate world. One of the most popular blog posts was entitled "How to live off £10 a day".

"My target was £10 a day. That's all money for food, transport, going out, clothes, toiletries etc (basically anything apart from rent and bills)."

Perhaps the thought of this is unacceptable to you or perhaps you're in a completely different financial league. However, for anyone serious about making the leap and worried about the finances, minimize your costs and you have options, keep spending and you'll carry on being stuck.

Here are some practical strategies for managing your spending:

- **Make a budget** – Be a geek, make a spreadsheet.

- **Strip back on everything** – Live life as simply as possible.

- **Give yourself a day off** – One day a week where you can spend more, gives you something to look forward to!

- **Avoid spending on brands** – They're more expensive and not going to change your life like changing your job could.

- **Hunt for discounts** – Start buying value food at the supermarket and keep an eye on the reduced aisle (sign up to www.money savingexpert.com emails).

- **Avoid public transport** – Walk or cycle (free and great exercise).

- **Avoid taking cash out** – If it's not in your wallet it's harder to spend it.

- **Make your own lunch** – Cheaper and now you can avoid going to the cashpoint altogether.

- **Save up for nights out** – This was the toughest part for Dom, but he found it possible to live on less than £10 a day which allowed him to "go crazy" on a couple of pints later in the week ("you'll be amazed at how sweet they tasted!").

- **Deal with rent** – Can you find a smaller apartment with less rent? If you've got a mortgage can you let it out and find somewhere cheaper? Can you think of creative short-term ways of paying no rent at all?

- **Move abroad** – Can you physically move yourself to somewhere where it is cheaper to live? Your escape fund might last you three times as long if you moved abroad (plus it could make things a lot more fun . . .).

How much do you want it?

I must admit it's not easy, and sustaining it is really hard, but I have found the whole experience strangely satisfying. Going from a bloke who never saved and never looked at his bank balance to the opposite is tough. But when my motivation is low I just remember that it will all be worth it when I finally escape the city. 9 weeks to go!

Dom Jackman – Escape the City Co-Founder, October 2009

esc Save intelligently

Adopt a system to help you save. This can be both a great discipline, and a source of motivation, as you watch your escape fund grow. Dom used this Three-Account Saving System:

Account A – Work out your fixed costs. What can you not live without? Rent, bills, phone bill were Dom's. Change the direct debits so they are all coming out of one account. This is Account A. Make sure there is enough cash to just cover those fixed costs a month (set up a standing order from Account C – see below).

Account B – Work out a budget. Use a second account to cover your monthly budget. Everything you buy during the month comes out of this account. Then you can go to the hole-in-the-wall and the balance will be how much cash you have left that month.

Account C – Have a third account where the rest of your salary goes. Hopefully you will see it rising towards your escape goal!

The sooner you start (even if you don't yet know what you're saving for) the sooner you'll have serious options. This was Dom's perspective: "I'm not going to lie – this is not exactly fun but I have realized that spending more money per day = more time in boring job. Budget wins every time."

Lloyds TSB bank in the UK has a feature called "Save the Change". Every time you use your debit card it rounds the transaction up to the nearest pound and deposits the difference in a savings account of your choice. Nifty automatic savings ideas like this are a good way to top up your Escape Fund on top of direct debits without requiring the discipline of manually moving the cash across.

Whatever you are saving for, just make sure it is aligned with your values. If you value adventure, save for a big road trip. If you value charity, save for a charitable project. If you value security, save for your house. If you value private education, save for your kid's school fees. If you value independence, save for your own business startup.

Esc

Previous attempts to save never seemed to work out as I could never figure out an easy way to track how much money I had at any given point in the month (given direct debits). However, I knew I needed to make this happen. The answer, I found, was to have three accounts instead of just one.

Dom Jackman – Escape the City Co-Founder, Oct 2009

esc Earn creatively

There are lots of ways to supplement your income (pre and post-escape). We've listed some ideas below, but it's not an exhaustive list. You'll have your own ideas too. All of these approaches will give you more options and a greater chance of making your career transition a success.

Part-time work

Sure you didn't get that degree (or two) plus all those years of professional experience to have to wait tables or pull pints. Consulting, contracting and tutoring are common ways for people with relevant skills to monetize their experience. Know how many days or hours a month you need to work in order to stay afloat.

Marketplace websites like odesk.com, 3desk.com and elance.com are great for putting your professional skills up for hire. And you can control the location, duration and rate of the work you choose to apply for. There are lots of offline recruitment agencies that specialize in part-time professionals. Sign up with a few in your industry.

Developing an online presence and a unique voice can be important for good consulting and contracting gigs.

Some people find part-time work a welcome break from "the main thing" and others find that it's a distraction. Rob certainly found it challenging preparing for his private tutoring lessons and thought that they broke the rhythm of focusing on Escape the City. That said, for £30 an hour it certainly wasn't to be sniffed at.

Rent stuff out

It is amazing what ingenious ways you can use to supplement your income. Rent things you own. You could sublet your bedroom on AirBnB and sleep on the sofa. Or you could let out your entire apartment and move in with friends or family. We have even heard of people renting out their residential car parking spaces.

Sell stuff

Although you're unlikely to afford many extra months of living by selling your shoes on Ebay, some extra pocket money never hurts. Besides, this could be a great opportunity to simplify your life in order to focus on your priorities. If you are fortunate enough to own any valuable assets this may be the right time to sell them. Dom's canoe is now very much an ex-possession!

Get paid for anything

If you're starting a business and have a world-beating business plan that you're working towards don't be worried about getting paid for something that you hadn't planned on getting paid for.

With Escape the City we are building a forward-looking professional network that connects talented people with opportunities that matter to them. We have ambitious plans for making money from using technology to scale these introductions. However, when someone calls us up and asks for a simple job advert on our site we certainly say yes. We have also made money since starting out by selling e-books and from dozens of events with inspirational speakers.

Be flexible. Earn creatively.

> *We made 500 [boxes of each cereal] (Obama O's and Cap'n McCains). [They] sold for $40 each. The Obama O's sold out, netting the funds we needed to keep AirBnB alive. The Cap'n McCains ... they didn't sell quite as well, and we ended up eating them to save money on food.*

Joe Gebbia – AirBnB co-founder

Avoid debt (or pay it down)

The best advice if you want to have lots of options with your career is not to get into debt in the first place. The next best advice is to eliminate debt as quickly as you can. And this often means staying in that corporate job, banking the salary, and getting debt-free as a matter of priority. For God's sake don't get a credit card!

When Mikey escaped the city to join our team he actually was in debt. He certainly has no sympathy for his previous self: "I had been earning at least £25k net income for the last 3 years, I SHOULD HAVE HAD NO DEBT. Sure I had a student loan, but I had no mortgage. That credit card debt meant I had certainly lived beyond my means . . ."

> **"** *Being in debt can feel like wearing boots of lead. It puts a mighty obstacle between ourselves and our dreams. It is a bondage. It ties us down. We make debt-repayment a priority and postpone the thing it is that we really want to do. Therefore, we end up staying in our slave-jobs. 'I hate my job and would love to quit,' people say, 'but I owe five grand to the bank, so I can't.' In this respect, debt has been compared by many to a modern form of indentured labour. You get into debt, and then you are stuck in a job you hate in order to pay off the debt.* **"**
>
> **Tom Hodgkinson – How To Be Free**

esc **Build assets, question liabilities**

Chris Guillebeau has an excellent section on personal finance in *The Art of Non-Conformity*. We have drawn heavily on his inspiration in our own escapes. Chris distinguishes between wealth-based financial independence (living off the interest or income on your financial assets) and income-based financial independence (replacing employer income with a certain amount of self-created income). What assets could you use your salary to develop? What additional income streams could you develop alongside your salary?

Be smart. If you are on a massive salary and you're really unhappy, live on a quarter of it and invest the remaining three-quarters in assets not liabilities. An asset is something that pays you money every year (paper investments, businesses, property), whereas a liability is something that you have to pay money towards.

We're not saying don't get a mortgage on a house and don't save for the future. But really assess your motives for doing either of these things and get clear on whether they're really helping you or not. Really consider before committing to anything that limits your choices. Be clear on why you are committing to it and whether it helps you get where you really want to be. If you do have a mortgage be sensible about it – live at home and rent out the entire property.

Pensions are a particularly sensitive subject. How many people do you know in their late 50s and early 60s who have diligently done what the system expected of them their whole careers, only to be screwed over just before they crossed the retirement line? The fallout from the recession has meant that many pension pots have taken a massive hit.

So many people who have worked in big companies for decades have carefully calculated the savings they'll have when they retire at 65, only to be laid off a few years short of the target. They're often too old to get a job anywhere else (they're too expensive) and they now face the prospect of a considerably less comfortable retirement than the one they had been counting on all those years.

> **"** *I have lost count of the successful, high-earning mid-dle-class couples I've met who choose to live in vast palaces financed by giant debts and then complain about the mortgage and money and the terrible suf-fering of their lives, as if they had no choice in the matter.* **"**
>
> **Tom Hodgkinson – How To Be Free**

Invest in yourself, not stuff

The two most constructive ways you can invest in yourself are through new experiences and education. You don't have to quit your job to do either of these.

D.H. Lawrence said that travel is the only thing you spend money on that makes you richer.

Rare is the person who returns from a genuinely new and adventurous experience without a fresh perspective on something they took for granted at home.

Learn. Use the library, beg, steal, download and borrow books. There really is no excuse for being uninformed about anything you consider important for your career transition.

We advocate spending consciously and spending on things that are important to you. Look your finances in the eye and then look your values in the eye. Decide how much you need and want (there's no wrong answer) for what you want to do. Then plan accordingly.

> *Old men are always advising young men to save money. That is bad advice. Don't save every nickel. Invest in yourself. I never saved a dollar until I was 40 years old.*
>
> **Henry Ford**

esc **Conclusion – The Money Question**

There is no single way to answer the Money Question. There is certainly no easy way. If living a life on your own terms was easy we'd all be doing it and there'd be no need for Escape the City or this book. It is important to remember that very few decisions are completely irreversible. You can always go back to your job.

If you know you need to earn at least £XX,000 per year in order to cover your needs (to survive) and your wants (to be happy) then you might dismiss the concept of escaping as impossible. We want to ask you to reframe the way you conceive of this word "escape". If you're unhappy in your job you have a duty to yourself, your family and the world to do something about it.

The boundaries around your Escape and the Money Question are completely up to you. The thing that unites you with everyone else reading this book is the fact that you are considering an escape of sorts. What matters is that you psychologically combine the desire for change with your personal financial situation. And that you're brutally honest with yourself on both fronts.

We were all brought up to follow instructions and play by the rules. Very few of us received a proper personal finance education. The result is that many of us feel completely ill equipped to live a life outside the security of a job. Be aware that a lot of the challenges you will face when escaping involve your own mentality with regards to money. Money is so tied up with our emotions, ego and pride that it can be hard to ask other people for help. You may not like the idea of no longer sitting in a certain place in the wealth pecking order of your friends. The simple answer here is usually that you have to swallow your pride, and take a long-term view. You have a plan, remember!

Money is the one force that is most likely to keep you spending five days a week doing work that doesn't matter to you. Give this subject the attention it deserves. There is a difference between a gamble and a plan. A gamble involves running *away from* something and resigning without a safety net or plan at all. A plan involves taking purposeful steps *towards* real change.

Broadly speaking, we all spend what we have. You just need to make sure that what you spend helps you get to where you want. You only have one life. There are many potential paths. The next chapter talks you through taking the first steps . . .

In the day-to-day trenches of adult life, there is actually no such thing as atheism. There is no such thing as not worshipping. Everybody worships. The only choice we get is what to worship. And the compelling reason for maybe choosing some sort of God or spiritual-type is that pretty much anything else you worship will eat you alive. If you worship money and things, if they are where you tap real meaning in life, then you will never feel you have enough.

David Foster Wallace – This Is Water *(2005)*

CHAPTER 5

EVOLUTION NOT REVOLUTION

This chapter is about transition – the specific process of deciding what you want to do and subsequently untangling yourself from your corporate job. This chapter hinges on making the decision to leave. The first half addresses the process of knowing you're keen to move but without being sure when or what for. The second half deals with that period in your job after you've resolved you're going to leave.

Our experiences of transitioning away from the corporate world can be summarized in three words: Learn, Experiment and Network. Escaping is a process not an event. Many of us think that you have to make a sudden leap, whereas it is far more sensible to take small steps. Do this and the transition will be less stressful and far more likely to last.

If you are anything like us you may have identified the blockers between you and the life you want. You may even have decided certain important things regarding your attitude towards work and life. However, it is very easy to get stuck on the difficult question of: "if not this, then what?" Furthermore, even once you've decided what you are going to change to you may be thinking: "how on earth do I actually make the transition?"

For Roz Savage, the simple act of writing two obituaries catalyzed a whole series of events that took her life in a radically different and unconventional direction. The important thing to realize is that even for her, it was "an evolution, not a revolution".

Before we start the transition chapter we'll let Roz tell the story of the next phase of her journey after her gradual epiphany that something had to change . . .

> *"One by one, I shed the trappings of my old life – the job, the husband, the home, the little red sports car. I moved house with increasing regularity, wherever I could find cheap or preferably free accommodation. I lived in a tiny cabin on a barge on the Thames, then a Dickensian garret in Richmond, then an office in Battersea.*
>
> *Every time I moved house I got rid of more stuff, the stuff that had been weighing me down, the stuff that I had allowed to own me rather than me owing it. I pared life down to the basics to find out what really mattered to me, to find out what was left when I was defined by what I was, not what I owned.*
>
> *Little by little I began to realign my life, to put myself on track for the obituary I really wanted. I learned that living life according to my values made me happier than a big income and lots of possessions. I stopped being a compulsive planner and started taking a more flexible approach to life. I stopped caring so much about what other people thought of me, and started caring more about what I thought of myself. I accepted that mistakes are a fact of life, an inevitable consequence of being adventurous and trying new things. I realized that it matters less whether something is a success or a failure, and matters more what I learn from the experience.*
>
> *It became clear to me, intellectually and emotionally and intuitively, that we have to look after our planet if we want it to look after us.*
>
> *I felt I was getting a few things figured out. But I was like a carpenter with a brand new set of tools, and no wood to work on. I needed a project.*
>
> *And so I decided to row the Atlantic."*
>
> **Roz Savage – www.rozsavage.com**

PRE-DECISION

"The voyage of the best ship is a zigzag line of a hundred tacks. See the line from a sufficient distance, and it straightens itself to the average tendency. Your genuine action will explain itself, and will explain your other genuine actions."

Ralph Waldo Emerson

esc Fight the fear

We knew we wanted to leave the corporate world and start a business. We still didn't have a business idea and we certainly didn't know when we were going to make the jump. It was extremely easy to allow the uncertainty and fear to paralyze us from taking even the first steps. In retrospect, if we hadn't been plotting to start a business together perhaps we would never have overcome the fear alone.

The core theme of our transition advice is not letting worries (the Thoughts and Blockers from Chapter 2) prevent you from taking the necessary first small steps.

Steven Pressfield, author of *The War of Art* calls this kind of paralyzing fear "The Resistance". He says that the more scared you are of a kind of work or calling, the surer you can be that you should try and do it. "To yield to Resistance deforms our spirit," he claims, "It stunts us and makes us less than we are and were born to be."

Is your fear rational or irrational? Fear serves us very well in lots of situations. It protects us from bad outcomes. However, we are often fearful of things that aren't genuine threats to our safety. For example, the fear of being embarrassed or the fear of public speaking.

Returning to Rob Archer's talk (from The Career Psychologist, www.thecareerpsychologist.com): "If you are scared of doing something, it is either helpful fear and you should listen to the reasons why you are afraid (and plan for them, problem solve them and manage the risks). Or it is unhelpful fear and you will be faced with a decision: accept the fear or change direction. In nearly all situations it is not a question of whether your fears are 'true' or not, but whether they are helpful to you."

Fear can be useful to warn you about a genuine danger but often it is paralyzing and based on a "what if" (i.e. a situation which isn't yet real). What if we can't write this book? What if everyone laughs at us when we make a speech? What if we fail? Well, firstly, define failure! Secondly, can you do anything about these kinds of fears? Ironically, listening to them makes the outcome you are scared of more likely.

Why is this relevant for your transition? Because fear is so powerful that it can actually stop you taking the first tiny steps required to get you to a place where you can even make a decision to escape.

There are a whole host of things you can consider – even before deciding to make a change – which will give you comfort both in terms of managing the risk and reducing your levels of fear. Taking a sabbatical whilst you try something new can be a great insurance policy. Saving an escape fund before you even know what it is for gives you options. Ultimately, you should remind yourself that this isn't an irreversible decision and that you can always go and get another job.

Courage is not the absence of fear, but rather the judgement that something else is more important than fear.

James Neil Hollingworth (1933–1996) – a beatnik, hippie, writer and manager of psychedelic folk rock bands. He wrote under the pseudonym Ambrose Redmoon

Enforce limits, push back

"Take the charity days!"

Dom used to say this to me, slapping his forehead for emphasis. What he meant was: "we have 25 days holiday a year, you can 'buy' an extra 6, and you get 2 charity volunteering days off work – take the charity days!"

Before we decided to leave our jobs we found it extremely important to protect ourselves from some of the excesses of the corporate world. It's very easy to find yourself working 70-hour weeks with little time left to consider your future.

Most of us can't afford to resign until we've got the new thing (job/startup) up and running. What we did was jealously guard our free time (making personal sacrifices of course) but we pushed back as much we could at work to give ourselves some breathing space.

Your employer is buying your time. They are paying you a certain amount of money in exchange for a certain amount of output. You can show them a certain amount of loyalty and you should expect a certain amount back. However, there are limits. Enforce those limits. You need to protect yourself and give yourself space to figure out whether you're going to leave or what you can do to improve your situation.

Certainly don't become one of those grumpy people who resents everything their managers ask them to do. Keep pretending everything is fine. You'll do yourself no favours by becoming resentful or obstructive – both in terms of your mentality and your reputation.

Beware a routine that blinkers you or exhausts you. You can't necessarily be objective about your life when you're in it. There is a life out there that doesn't involve your current situation. You just can't always see it from where you're sitting. If you do find yourself in the unfortunate position of being laid off, embrace the dead time. See it as an opportunity. You sometimes need to find space to breathe, regroup and assess your options.

I remember after the first month in India, sitting on the beach, taking in a deep breath and feeling like a little piece of me had come back. You don't realize how broken you are until you take a step back.

Rekha Mehr – entrepreneur, baker

esc Get better at listening

Question: How do I learn, experiment and network?
Answer: Get better at listening. Listen first; then act.

When you're stuck in a job you don't like, you're driving yourself up the wall with your internal voice. You're talking yourself out of every potential constructive forward action. You are stuck in a loop. You need to get out of it. You need to expose yourself to new ideas.

Before we came up with the idea for Escape the City, Rob was so demo-tivated by his corporate job that he found himself spending a fair bit of time reading blogs about things that interested him – the challenges the world faces in the 21st century, innovative business models and exciting startups (as well as Manchester United of course . . .).

In fact, the single thing that catalyzed the whole voyage of discovery for Rob was when he stumbled across a fascinating free online PDF called The IdeaVirus whilst researching call centre customer service for work. The more he read about entrepreneurialism, the more he realized what a massive mismatch there was between the world he was working in and the world he was reading about. The direction of his escape was becom-ing clearer.

What can you do to get better at listening? Get the spreadsheet of every TED talk ever recorded (just Google "TED talks spreadsheet"),[1] mark the ones that interest you and watch one a day until you decide to quit your job! Straightaway this evening you can set yourself up with a Feedly account and a Twitter account and begin following people who interest you.

What is Feedly? Every blog and most websites have an RSS feed. You copy the URL and paste it into the "subscribe" field in your Feedly account. This is your personalized news feed. You can now subscribe to anyone with a perspective that interests you and you never have to go back to their website to get their latest updates. For those of you who are interested in startups we'd recommend www.sethgodin.com, www.chrisbrogan.com and www.avc.com as great places to start. You could also subscribe to

our blog ("Stop Dreaming, Start Planning") with the RSS link http://
blog.escapethecity.org/feed/. Check out the bibliography at the back of
this book for all the blogs we subscribe to.

There are fascinatingly interesting people and ideas and conversations
happening **right now** online. Ten years ago you would never have had
access to this information and now you can get it all on your mobile
phone. This is an excellent post by an Escape the City member who finally
"got" Twitter: http://www.giveliveexplore.com/2012/10/11/the-power-
of-twitter-told-in-3-tweets/.

What does this have to do with your escape? Everything. You are not
going to enjoy any new job or startup unless you are genuinely interested in the subject matter. We all have unique combinations of interests
and skills. The future career path that you are going to walk down will
exist somewhere at the intersection of your interests, your skills, your
network and your experiences.

The more you can develop all of these areas the more likely you are to
find and create opportunities that really resonate with you.

> *Nobody made a bigger mistake than he who did
> nothing because he could do only a little.*

Edmund Burke – Irish statesman, political theorist

esc Stop reading, start acting

There comes a point where you have to stop being a voyeur and start taking part. What might this consist of? Well, at first, it certainly doesn't involve just quitting your job. At first it might just involve taking some really modest steps.

For us it first involved speaking to some entrepreneur friends with an online education business about how to build a website. Our next step was to actually start our own blog (anonymously) where we began discussing the idea of building a community of corporate escapees.

You don't need to know what direction you are heading in at this stage. The steps might be as simple as coming along to the next Escape the City event or requesting a meeting with a friend in another industry to talk about their job. Whatever the steps are, approach them with an open mind and ask lots of questions.

Here are some ideas based on our experiences:

Idea 1: Expose yourself to new networks

Identify different communities that you might be interested in. Use Meetup.com and Eventbrite.com to track down events that look interesting to you. Go to these events. Be brave. Take a friend. Engage people in conversation. Use Lanyrd.com to get a summary of the events that anyone you follow on Twitter is going to.

Idea 2: Find your voice

Once you're getting confident with the process of discovering new niches and new worlds, perhaps it's time to start projecting some of yourself out into the world? Start a blog (don't worry, no one is going to be reading it yet). Write some articles. Delete them if you feel uncomfortable. What could you read about all day? What could you write a well-informed article about?

Idea 3: Build your own mini-tribe

If you're comfortable with the direction your career is heading in why not start organizing your own meet-ups in the pub after work? Whatever it is that you might want to go and do there will be people who feel the same way. Assemble a group of women who want to build online businesses, or of financial traders who want to work in social businesses, or of accountants who want to volunteer in Africa. What we did was we began organising the London tribe of corporate escapees. You're only reading this book because we took those first steps.

Idea 4: Embark on a series of escape experiments

Take a day of holiday and shadow a friend around their job. Write to five business owners in areas that interest you and ask them whether you can interview them for an article/research project. Volunteer with a local charity or community organization. Instead of casting around for that "one thing" that will save you from the corporate grind, you should explore many different avenues and pursue those that interest you. The key is to start.

*   *   *

We've already told you about Piers Calvert – the South American photographer. Although he had been improving his photography skills whilst still in his job, his escape really started when he took a single, random photograph . . .

He was flying into London early one morning and, 10 minutes before landing at Heathrow, he took a few pictures of London buried under fog with only Canary Wharf's skyscrapers emerging above it. Upon arrival he emailed one picture to a couple of friends to illustrate his observation about how grey and miserable London was.

The photo went viral and the next day was picked up by the evening news and published in the national press. It then went on to win an award in a high profile photography competition at the Natural History Museum. Piers told us that that was it – the sign that he needed.

Don't get downhearted by the thought that so many peoples' paths seem to be relatively haphazard, be energized by the thought that you don't need a guidebook for an unconventional career. Just focus on learning, starting small projects and engaging in **new** conversations that interest you. Do this and be alive to new possibilities.

Pamela Slim talks about how important it is psychologically for people in corporate jobs, who may have huge fears about making movement, to do small tests . . .

> **"** Imagine you're standing on a high diving board and you're looking down at the water. If you stare down at the water for an hour, your anxiety is going to increase the longer you're standing there, right? So the key is to get people in the water as soon as possible **"**
>
> **Pamela Slim – in a Forbes interview with Eric Wagner[2]**

POST-DECISION

"Plan it thoroughly. If it feels right, and you know it's right, take the plunge and go for it. Speak to people in the know. Glean them (subtly and politely) for information. Learn from them. Learn everything you can about your field."

Frank Yeung – Co-Founder Poncho8 Gourmet Burritos, ex-Goldman Sachs

`esc` Don't quit just yet

So you've decided you're going to leave . . .

Firstly, congratulations! Seriously. Many of us stay in the pre-decision cycle for years (if not forever). If you're in a position to decide that you're going to leave – even if you don't know what you're going to do next – celebrate the exciting feeling of knowing that change is coming your way. The next few pages cover that exciting and terrifying period in between resolving to leave and the moment you walk out of those doors for the last time.

You may work in an environment that is genuinely doing you no good at all but even though you probably need to get out of there as soon as possible, you still need to be careful that you're not just running away from something. Once you've made the decision that you're going to leave . . . what do you do next? You need a plan!

Way before actually resigning Scott Gilmore, founder of Open Markets, spoke to other people who had launched their own charity or social enterprise: "from them I got the sense that this would be hard, but it was possible". He also spoke with his father, a successful entrepreneur, and obtained his guidance and advice about how to start and grow a business.

Once Jon Warren made his mind up to escape private wealth client management he stopped standing outside the office with the smokers talking about how he was going to move to Spain and set up a business. Instead he started putting together ideas and business plans during his lunch break. He now runs his own food company on the Bay of Biscay called San Sebastian Food, creating unique food and wine experiences.

Unless your plan is to quit without a plan (i.e. to give yourself breathing space or to go on a big adventure), KEEP YOUR JOB! The most sure-fire way to end up back in another corporate job that drives you up the wall within six months is to quit without knowing what you're going to do or without enough of a financial safety net. Remember Roz Savage's advice – evolution not revolution.

> **"** *Even though I've said, 'Do stuff after hours. Don't quit your job,' when people write to me and say, 'I quit my job.' I say, 'No. No. No. No. No.' For all the hype, I'm obnoxiously practical.* **"**
>
> **Gary Vaynerchuk – entrepreneur**

Just start (but start small)

One of the first things we learnt when we decided to build Escape the City was that whatever idea, plan or project you are working on, the only real way to know if something is worth pursuing is by actually starting it. This doesn't mean that you have to risk your shirt on an unproven concept. It just means that you should get the ball rolling. What are the three actions you could take by the end of this week that would get you a few steps closer to knowing something you don't know today about your potential next move?

The "just start" advice is borrowed from Innocent's book: *A Book About Innocent: Our Story and Some Things we've Learned*. They combined it with the "start small". It's golden advice.

The (now legendary) story saw the three of them setting up a market stall at a London jazz festival. They were giving away homemade all-fruit smoothies (something that didn't really exist in England at that time). They put up a sign saying "Should we give up our day jobs to make these smoothies?" They had one bin that said YES and another that said NO. No prizes for guessing which one was full by the end of the weekend.

We applied the "start small" advice at the end of August 2009 when we sat on a park bench in Wimbledon, drank a beer in the setting sun, and agreed to start the Escape blog. Little did we know at the time, but that decision would unleash a domino effect of ideas and progress and connections and karma that has led to us to writing this book . . . building a worldwide community and helping thousands of other people find exciting career opportunities, start businesses and go on big adventures.

Until one is committed, there is hesitancy, the chance to draw back, always ineffectiveness. Concerning all acts of initiative (and creation), there is one elementary truth, the ignorance of which kills countless ideas and splendid plans: that the moment one definitely commits oneself, then Providence moves too. All sorts of things occur to help one that would never otherwise have occurred. A whole stream of events issues from the decision, raising in one's favour all manner of unforeseen incidents and meetings and material assistance, which no man could have dreamt would have come his way. I learned a deep respect for one of Goethe's couplets:

Whatever you can do or dream you can, begin it.

Boldness has genius, power and magic in it!

William Hutchinson Murray (1913–1996) – from his book The Scottish Himalayan Expedition

Test towards the way that works

Returning to our theme of treating your career transition like a startup. When you're building a startup you have assumptions and requirements. The assumptions are the bets you are making about your product (i.e. people will find this feature useful, people will be prepared to pay for this, etc.) and the requirements are the broad goals or criteria that the product has to achieve to tie in with your vision (i.e. we are starting this business in order to help demographic X do Y).

The best entrepreneurs don't spend months building products in order to find out whether their assumptions are true. They go straight out to speak to potential customers to figure out whether their hunches are right. This is a very basic description of the Lean Startup Movement – a scientific approach to creating and managing startups by eliminating wasted time and money. See: www.theleanstartup.com/principles.

The exact same principles can be applied to your career transition. You need to figure out your requirements (i.e. the non-negotiable – or partly negotiable – requirements of the vision for your escape). These are your decision criteria. You also need to get clear on your assumptions (your unanswered questions). This can save you a lot of time heading down the wrong path.

An example escape assumption might be: "I'm sure there is demand for my financial modelling skills in social enterprises – I think I'd be able to get a job in a top online social enterprise on a salary not dissimilar to my current one." The traditional way of going about this would be to apply to every social enterprise job you can find, spend hours tailoring cover letters so that it seems like you're a good fit for the role, take time off work to attend interviews – only to discover at the end of the process that you never really stood a chance because you don't have the right skill set or are too expensive.

The sensible Lean Startup approach to this would have been to use Linkedin to identify someone doing the job you think you'd like to do. First of all, can you ascertain whether they've got a similar career background to you? Secondly, do you have any shared connections through which you could request an introduction? If so, can you write a very brief, very polite email that asks the person for five minutes on the phone to ask for some career advice?

The chances are that all it will take is a brief phone call to ask some well-thought out questions that will either give you the confidence you need to proceed, the advice you need to adjust your approach, or the answers you need to know to decide that this path isn't worth pursuing.

In any escape – whether it is to a new job or to start a business – you should test your basic assumptions before investing lots of time or money in the plan and without exposing yourself to unnecessary levels of risk by quitting.

> *If you don't know what you're testing, all the results in the world will tell you nothing.*

Eric Ries – The Lean Startup

`esc` **Create a checklist**

Everything we've learnt since quitting our jobs, and speaking to thousands of people who have done the same, about figuring out what you should go and do can be summarized by this advice: "keep placing small bets, make sure you have the right checklist of pre-escape questions and only quit when you can say 'yes' to everything on the list."

Steve Reid started his career as an accountant, and then worked in finance at IMG media, before finally joining the Internet startup mydeco. He came up with the idea for Tribesports.com whilst training for Ironman France with a friend. Steve took a sensible approach and continued working the day job for another 18 months, learning as much as he could from those around him.

The entrepreneurs he spoke to before resigning ran him through a series of questions to make sure he was clear what he was letting himself in for. Can you make a checklist of the things you need to be able to answer "yes" to in order to resign?

- *Are you solving a real problem?*
- *Do you have your family's support?*
- *Are you in a financial position to not have a salary for as long as it takes?*
- *Are you willing to sacrifice what most people take for granted to make your business a success, putting normal life on hold?*
- *Are you prepared for a lonely journey?*
- *Are you resilient enough to listen to no's and doubters, but stay headstrong?*
- *Do you care about your users and business so much it is like your baby – you'd do anything for it? Have you got great co-founders that share your passion?*

Steve Reid– co-founder Tribesports.com

esc Cultivate partners-in-crime

None of us would have been able to start Escape the City by ourselves. We were extremely fortunate in that we met at a time when we were keen to start a business. The idea developed between us. We encouraged each other to the edge of the plank. Resigning together meant that the whole thing had that much more momentum and it would be that much harder to listen to the fear and back out.

Although it is tempting to seek out gurus and mentors, don't underestimate the power of hanging out with people at your level. They know what you're going through and can really relate to your situation. If you're starting a business, find other people at your stage (i.e. people starting businesses, not those already running profitable businesses). Can you form a club of peers to meet one evening a month to talk about your startups?

Matt Trinetti is an Escape the City member in Chicago who wanted to explore new career options and business ideas. He and some friends formed a book club to discuss ideas that they weren't interacting with at work. The books they read covered the latest ideas in career development and entrepreneurial business. You can follow the adventures that this buddying process has sparked for Matt at www.giveliveexplore.com.

Try to surround yourself with people who are interested in the same things as you. If you spend all week with people who don't enjoy their jobs and your evenings in pubs moaning about work you'll probably dislike your job even more. However, if you start spending time with people doing interesting things with their lives, perhaps you'll also follow suit? Find your tribe.

The old ways are dead. And you need people around you who concur. That means hanging out more with the creative people, the freaks, the real visionaries, than you're already doing. Thinking more about what their needs are, and responding accordingly. Avoid the dullards; avoid the folk who play it safe. They can't help you anymore. Their stability model no longer offers that much stability. They are extinct, they are extinction.

***Hugh Macleod* – How To Be Creative**

Reframe the risk

Dom rationalized his resignation in the following way: "If I was to tell people I was leaving to do a Masters the conversations I'd be having would all be about how much I'll learn and how it was a good, safe option. But exactly the same goes for startups. Even if it fails, I'll learn more trying to start a business than I have ever done doing anything so far and I won't have to pay tuition fees."

Dom could easily have spent two years getting into debt chasing another qualification and it wouldn't have been seen as a big risk. So he began thinking about starting a business differently. It was like a Masters he wasn't going to pay for and if it failed, he could simply find a new job.

Once we'd had the idea, we weren't prepared to carry on in our jobs with the nagging "what if's", never knowing whether we'd have been able to pull it off. Both of us called Escape the City a project and a community before we ever called it a business. In this way, and especially before we resigned, we were playing a subtle mind-trick on ourselves – removing some of the pressure.

Rather than thinking about the risks of making a change, perhaps you should ask yourself what the risk is of not doing what you really want to do with your life?

> " *So my final piece of advice is this: when faced with the choice between engaging with reality or engaging with what Erich Fromm calls the 'necrophiliac' world of wealth and power, choose life, whatever the apparent costs may be.* "
>
> **George Monbiot – Journalist**

Resign (carefully)

The final step in any escape is the fateful moment of resignation. Once you've made the decision to leave you then have to decide when to resign. Ideally you'll hand in your notice when you can answer "yes" to all of the questions on your checklist. You may decide to leave when you hit the target in your Escape Fund.

It is often hard to take the final step. Not that we would advise following his example but Rob resigned because his annual review came around and he had decided not to spend the previous three weeks doing the necessary work of collecting feedback from all his managers. Rather than handing over a dossier of references in the meeting with his director he handed in his notice. He had essentially forced himself into a decision by not preparing for the annual review.

Most of the resignations we've heard about have taken place without incident. The worrying about it is often way worse than the reality. Be prepared to defend your decision if challenged and if you're happy with your plan don't be talked out of it. You will be surprised how positively many bosses react.

A word of caution: obviously you want to maintain a professional reputation and behave just like you'd expect an employee of yours to behave. What's more, you never know whether your colleagues and bosses could become future clients, useful contacts or even whether you might need to ask them for a job again one day! Don't burn any bridges.

Just after resigning and just before asking for a reference Rob made the mistake of sending an email to his director with some feedback explaining some of the reasons he and other people at his level were considering leaving. Big mistake. No reply, no reference!

Gareth Jenkins, a trainee accountant who was sacked from his Big 4 Accountancy job for failing his exams, far outdid Rob's well intended email with a cynical rant about corporate jargon that went viral and made it into the UK press. Needless to say, even though we doubt he wants a "City" job in future, he probably could have done without the notoriety that his email sparked. Read Gareth's email here: http://bit.ly/WkhFSE.

 But if anybody else wants to come with me, this moment will be the ground floor of something real and fun and inspiring and true in this godforsaken business and we will do it together! Who's coming with me besides . . . 'Flipper' here?

Tom Cruise as Jerry Maguire[3] – TriStar Pictures

Don't expect a bunch of roses

Ajit Chambers left banking to create a company that takes people on tours of disused London underground stations. He told us that the worst part of breaking free was that the people who really should support you are the first to bet against you.

It goes without saying that it's important that people who rely on you (or those you rely on) know what you are planning and that you bring them in on the decision-making process. However, ultimately, this is your decision and you may need to be prepared for resistance from your friends and family. Often this will come from well-meaning concerns about your security and a desire to protect you from failure.

What people may not realize is that you might *want* to take on challenges where you face the prospect of failure. Because that means you're trying something worth succeeding at. The people in your life have a mental framework for you. When you make significant changes you are no longer the person they knew before – thereby threatening their perception of you.

There's very little you can do about this other than asking for support, and letting your actions prove them wrong. It's also crucial that you protect yourself from pessimists and cynics, especially if they are close to you. You are entering into a period of your life where your self-confidence and morale may fluctuate wildly and you'll need all the support and stability you can get.

If your colleagues or friends are feeling frustrated with their own jobs or careers they may resent you precisely because you represent the changes that they are feeling unable to make – for whatever reason . . . "Oh, Mary can do that because X, Y, Z" or "Have fun saving the world Jim, some of us have to earn a living".

When you resign don't expect everyone to be thrilled for you. When Mikey resigned, the head of his department (the guy he had just given four years of hard work to and been for drinks with) didn't even look up from his desk and muttered "See you later then". Your escape may represent an alternative route to the path that more senior people have followed. It can feel like a smack in the face to someone who has spent their whole lives working for one company.

However, there will also be people who whisper to you in the corridor – "well done, good luck!" and "I wish I had the guts to do the same". All three of us received warm-hearted emails from colleagues wishing us luck.

The best way to get approval is not to need it. This is equally true in art and business. And love. And sex. And just about everything else worth having.

Hugh MacLeod – www.gapingvoid.com

Conclusion – Evolution Not Revolution

Quitting is often harder than sticking. There is a negative stigma around quitting. Like it's the easy option. Like you couldn't stick it out. The reality is that it is often far easier to keep cruising along. You don't have to worry about the big questions: "What could I do instead?" "How will I afford to live?" What should really have a negative stigma is staying in a situation that isn't right, for fear of facing the unknown.

Expose yourself to serendipity. Inspiration can come from anywhere. You can't know what you're looking for unless you know what is out there. Most people don't really have a clue what else is out there. Listen and learn first, then act. You don't yet know what you don't know. Read masses, watch TED talks, go to events, network with new people and discover what else there is – out there.

Once you're clear on the principles of your direction (remember, you don't have to know the specific job you're after and it doesn't have to be forever) you can set about finding opportunities within the broad area you're targeting. This is a fantastic position to be in. You're ahead of most people who are still stuck on "what on earth should I be doing?" Successful escapees just do lots of things that interest them. Some of it sticks and some of it falls away as valuable experience.

So hopefully by now you're getting your head around your transition. You're either looking for a new job, starting your own business, or you may even go on a big adventure before deciding on your next move. The following three chapters address each of these Escape Routes.

Bugle calls to quit a job you hate are not always realistic. Drum-beating shouts to do this and that are not for everybody. A more subtle change of tack may be more appropriate. Soften it, mould it to your own circumstances. But hold this one thing clear, whatever your situation: this is your life and you have the right to live it well. With rights come responsibilities, but you cannot do full justice to your commitments; to your family, your business, bank manager or parole officer, if you are not content. If you feel that you are not able, or not bold enough, to take giant leaps, take a small step. If you feel anxious about the consequences of changing the equilibrium, if you feel lost or beyond changing, take a tiny step and test the waters. We walk with small steps at first.

Alastair Humphreys – Ten Lessons From The Road

PART TWO

POST-ESCAPE

CHAPTER 6
FIND AN EXCITING JOB

Finding an exciting job is a massively subjective process. Many of the problems that you might face in your career will come about because you inherit other peoples' notions of what makes an exciting job. The world is a busy and competitive place and it's getting more so. If you don't enjoy your job you're unlikely to be able to compete with people who do. So it's important to make your choices your own. You'll do this by clarifying your principles and identifying your decision criteria.

Additionally, the sooner you accept that there aren't perfect jobs waiting on job boards for you, the sooner you can get on with the far more realistic task of building a career around your strengths, engaging with problems that interest you and developing skills that make you personally fulfilled. In this way you will eventually develop passions – often in areas you could never have predicted when you were deciding on a particular path. So give yourself a break and take the pressure off.

There are a lot of unhelpful myths regarding dream jobs, following passions, how to find opportunities, how to apply for jobs and how to succeed in interviews. The objective of this chapter is to talk you through what we have learnt about the process of job-hunting and how to give yourself the best chance of success. Although the messages are

Esc

particularly relevant if you work in a big corporate, a lot of the advice is more broadly applicable.

> *If you tell yourself that your job has to be something you'd do even if you didn't get paid, you'll be looking for a long time. Maybe forever.*

Penelope Trunk – founder of Brazen Careerist

esc Work is changing

You may not see your job as a series of projects, but that is all most jobs are. And amazing things come from projects . . .

Kelly Cheesman is a fantastic front-end developer currently working with us in London. She is from New Zealand. She had never been to Europe before, let alone the UK, when she accepted an offer to join us in London. She had been freelancing for Escape for 12 months prior to receiving the offer. She would never have been in a position to find an opportunity like this in London from New Zealand had she not being working for us on a project basis beforehand.

We began seeing our jobs through the lens of our employer buying our time (i.e. projects that just happened to be full-time). Thinking about our job in terms of an hourly wage was very interesting. We added up how much time we spent commuting and how much time we spent at work in a year. We calculated our hourly wage. The salary may have been considerable but our average hourly earnings were about £13 an hour. This depressing realization prompted the question of what was important to us – time or money? And on what terms for both?

In retrospect we've realized how searching for the perfect, linear career progression – promotion to promotion, salary rise to salary rise – is a sure-fire way to guarantee never finding unconventional, entrepreneurial or exciting projects. At the time we couldn't see it. We were so used to jumping through hoops, not realizing that in order to find work that mattered to us we were going to have to go sideways, downwards, all over the place.

Hopefully the future of work will see more control in the hands of the individual rather than the employer. We recently spoke to Tom Savage, founder of the freelancer network 3desk.com, who told us how he hopes the employment landscape is shifting for the better. "Imagine a liquid market for talent, in which everyone knows their value. A market in which people choose who they work for, when they work and for how much."

Tom thinks that the recession, technological advances and increased mobility are some of the main forces driving these changes. They won't happen overnight, for sure, but if you're cynical about the rate of change just reflect on the widespread practice of "working from home" – which would have been unthinkable 10 years ago.

The idea of a job-for-life is already over. Perhaps soon the idea of a single employer owning all of your time will be a thing of the past for a lot of people. Corporate job security and employee loyalty are both pretty shaky. Perhaps you should start seeing yourself as a one-person business. What values do you represent? What impressions do you project? What do people think when they see you (online or in person)? How can you project an image that balances the work you want to do with what you can offer?

People are already building working lives on their own terms. You may just not be able to see them from your current conventional environment. They're in cafes, museums and libraries during the day. They're asleep or drinking coffee when you're battling the rush hour.

Sheena Matheiken is a freelance digital creative director who recently gave an interview on freelancing: "I seriously don't know why more people aren't doing this. I know too many talented people stuck at unhappy full-time gigs under the false pretext of security or comfort or whatever they rationalize it to be."[1]

The future is here already; you just may not be living it yet. Push a little. Investigate other peoples' working lives. You might be surprised what you discover.

 The future is about gigs and assets and art and an ever-shifting series of partnerships and projects. This revolution is at least as big as the last one, and the last one changed everything.

Seth Godin – author, entrepreneur, blogger

esc Get clear on your decision criteria

Throughout this book we encourage you to view your escape as a startup. This comparison applies not only to the financial side of things but to the vision and the core principles of your approach. What is your vision? What are the non-negotiable elements of your escape? What are the key ingredients for your new career?

Just like any good startup, the tactics of your escape will change (must change) but the overall principles should stay the same. These might be as broad as "I'd like to do my own thing", "I would like to work in a more client-facing job", or "I'd like do something with a positive social impact".

We've structured all the listings on Escape the City across five main "Escape Factors":

1. Entrepreneurial Work

2. Positive Social Impact

3. Exciting Brands

4. Exotic Locations

5. Adventurous Challenges

You might have considerably different Escape Factors. You might prioritize flexible working or a rural location above everything else. Or you could decide that your escape has to centre around something creative or a job where you don't have to sit in front of a computer all day. Whatever your priorities, you should begin to crystallize an idea of the ingredients you want your escape to include.

Your decision criteria will provide you with a map to navigate all the thousands of potential opportunities and different paths you could go down. It will be a huge relief to close down some avenues of enquiry and focus your escape.

Values and strengths tests can be helpful in order to narrow down your search. However, ultimately try to avoid using online tests to tell you what you should "be when you grow up". Coaches, mentors or friends can provide useful sounding boards for analyzing yourself objectively. The overall direction and decision has to come from you.

Esc

What are the non-negotiable features of your next career move? They don't have to be specific industries or job titles. Think in terms of the principles you want to work on, your financial ambitions, the environment you'd like to work in and the location. Not every job will tick every box but if you define your decision criteria you'll be able to narrow your search and you'll be better equipped to spot the "right" opportunity when you see it.

Which of these matter to you?

- Where you work.
- When you work.
- What you work on.
- How much you get paid.
- How much control you have.
- How much you learn every day.
- Who you work with.

Once you've worked out the broad vision for your career transition, like any startup in search of its business model, you should vigorously test and experiment till you find the context that works for you.

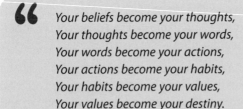

> *Your beliefs become your thoughts,*
> *Your thoughts become your words,*
> *Your words become your actions,*
> *Your actions become your habits,*
> *Your habits become your values,*
> *Your values become your destiny.*

Mahatma Gandhi

esc Forget passions, what can you offer?

We have been customers our whole lives. We have been customers of our schools, our parents, our universities and even our employers. This attitude towards the people and institutions in our lives can lead to a rather entitled view of the world. This section encourages you to start thinking like a supplier – not what can you receive but what can you offer?

We've already touched on challenges to the "Passion Hypothesis" (i.e. the idea that you have a pre-existing passion waiting to be discovered). Cal Newport takes the idea a step further in his new book, *So Good They Can't Ignore You*. He says that every time work gets hard too many of us have an existential crisis and ask ourselves an unanswerable question: "Is this what I'm really meant to be doing?" He suggests that this can lead to never putting in the hard graft of actually getting good at a job before freaking out and deciding to change.

He suggests that it is only through building valuable skills over time that you can really develop a sense of fulfilment (and potentially, eventually, passion). If he is right – and these points certainly make a lot of sense as so many people are stuck in the "what am I meant to do with my life?" eddy – then the most important thing you could be considering on your job hunt is: "what useful skills could I offer a prospective employer?"

Becoming useful inevitably leads to more responsibility, more interesting challenges and hopefully the satisfying levels of mastery that come with doing a job to an extremely high standard. The psychologist Mihaly Csikszentmihalyi proposed a mental state called "Flow" to describe a pleasurable state of single-minded immersion in a task that you can perform to a high standard even though it is quite challenging.

Why is this relevant? Because fulfilment, flow, or even passion cannot be predicted by reading a job listing or learning about a new industry. These highly sought after things can only evolve through the process of committing to a given field (preferably a field you are interested in) and investing the requisite time and effort in getting really good at something. In his book *Outliers*, Malcolm Gladwell suggested that it takes 10,000 hours to truly master a skill. You're going to have to be patient.

Esc

"Seek your passion" is dangerous advice that pre-supposes you have already put in the graft required to even be in a position to allow that passion to develop. How do you get yourself to a place where you can discover these things? Stop assessing what an employer might give you, start wondering what it is you could offer, and then put in the effort required to make yourself relevant and useful.

Does this mean that you should just pick the nearest career and work for five years being useful before knowing whether or not you've made the right choice? Definitely not. You should still adopt the "start small and experiment" approach. However, be aware that eventually you're going to have to choose something to commit to (even if it's becoming something varied, like an excellent wide-ranging digital freelance consultant) and once you've committed – relax if the new gig doesn't rock your world before you've even understood it.

> *To other young people who constantly wonder if the grass might be greener on the other side of the occupational fence, I offer this advice: Passion is not something you follow. It's something that will follow you as you put in the hard work to become valuable to the world.*

Cal Newport[3] – in the New York Times, 29 September 2012

Get your head around "skills"

We've already discussed the trap of collecting qualifications and the fact that so many escapes stall as a result of insecurities about skills. Developing new skills and reframing existing ones is obviously crucial in the context of a career transition.

The first thing to challenge is the confusion between skills and qualifications. Too many of us still think that in order to develop new skills we need to take more tests – another CFA exam or another legal qualification. If you want to transition away from big corporates, informal skills are far more important than external labels.

When Mikey moved back to New York in 2011 to launch Escape the City in the USA, he enrolled on a one-hour long Skillshare class on PR. It cost him $15. By the end of the session he had not only heard some great advice from someone who was passionate about PR and startups, he had been able to ask questions directly relating to his goal (getting coverage for his startup) and he had also met 30 other people with interesting stories who could open up new networks to him.

Here are the three things we believe about skills:

Lesson 1: New employers want proof of commitment far more than they need to see specific skills

Certain careers require specific qualifications as pre-requisites for consideration. If you definitely know that you want to get into such an area you may need to make a longer-term commitment to re-skilling. However, for many employers it's simply about commitment.

Escape the City has a good relationship with Prospectus, the third sector recruitment agency. Francesca Lahiguera, a director, told us how they often hear from private sector candidates regarding exciting charity jobs. They're always thrilled to receive such applications and although they assess whether the skill set is applicable, what they really want is proof of prior interest in the new area. If the candidate can't demonstrate commitment it is often a sign that they've simply had a bad week at work and applied on a whim. They're unlikely to be a good long-term fit.

So it's as much about doing things that demonstrate commitment (volunteering, side-projects, mentoring, trusteeships, etc.) as it is about needing a list of specific skills. Besides, through the process of showing commitment to a new area you will inevitably develop new skills as well.

Lesson 2: Developing new skills doesn't require quitting your job and can be a lot of fun

If you're in the pre-decision transition phase of your escape you may find yourself developing new skills before you even know what you need them for. Proactively adding strings to your bow is one way of sparking new interests and opening new doors without having to over-commit to anything.

The education industry is undergoing a revolution in terms of how information is distributed. In the past most knowledge was locked up in universities and libraries. Today the Internet is facilitating a massive democratization of knowledge. However, this is useless unless we know what to do with it.

A great place to start would be one of the 21st century campuses that are popping up all over the place. Offline you should check out www.generalassemb.ly (London, New York and increasingly everywhere), www.skillshare.com, www.hubacademy.com in London (there are Hubs – social enterprise focus – all around the world). Online universities include www.udacity.com, www.udemy.com and www.khanacademy.org.

The main change is that you no longer have to enrol on a three-year degree in order to develop a new skill. The risk in learning something new is much lower. Sure, these courses and classes may not carry the same external validation as an MBA or a degree, but ask yourself what you are studying for – the label or the knowledge?

If you're lucky you may find your own employer offers training courses in areas relevant to your escape plan. Lots of big corporates certainly have subscriptions to databases like Mintel (for market research), Gorkana (for PR and journalist contacts) and GetAbstract (for summaries of business books). You should definitely make the most of these resources while you're there.

Lesson 3: Your skills are way more transferable than you realize

Most jobs require generalists. A safe pair of hands. Someone with a track record of "getting things done". It often doesn't matter what your skills or experience are as long as you can point to proof of delivery. What you do need to do if you're selling your non-specific skills is tell a story that makes your past relevant for the new role that you are targeting. Besides, do you really want to work for an employer who isn't going to hire you unless you tick off every bureaucratic bullet point on their list of skill requirements?

You may want to hunt for opportunities to do a job similar to yours in a completely new sector. Look at the org chart of any organization, most have pretty similar roles no matter what the industry. If you no longer want to do your job function you simply need to make a case for moving sideways into a related area. For example, from finance you can often transition into operations. Work in a sales role? You could probably put a case for moving into the marketing team. Everything is negotiable. It's up to you to put the case for it.

* * *

After a four-year stint investment banking at Citigroup Trupti Patel found herself wondering what to do next. She now works at Social Finance, the UK's leading social finance social enterprise – where she can apply her professional and financial skills to a cause she is passionate about.

She explained how she didn't have a single moment of truth. Instead she had a series of experiences that led her down her new path. As part of her associate programme at Citigroup, she undertook a six-month rotation to their Sydney office. Six months in a different country and working environment where so much emphasis was placed on the work–life balance pushed her to finally quit her job back in London . . .

"I undertook some voluntary work in India on my time off, where I encountered a nun running an orphanage in the remote desert region. The nun was Oxford-educated and had grown a simple school into a full-blown school and college campus. That made me realize that I could use my financial skills in a social setting."

We should have more trust in our own resilience and less confidence in our predictions about how we'll feel. We should be a bit more humble and a bit more brave.

Elizabeth Gilbert – *author of* Eat, Pray, Love

esc Hunt people not jobs

Why is it all about relationships?

Apparently you are more likely to find your next opportunity through your friend's friend rather than your immediate network. Mark Granovetter, a sociologist at Stanford University, argues that "weak ties" are especially useful in the modern world.[4] Nicholas Christakis and James Fowler support this view in their book *Connected*, suggesting that it is through your widespread network of contacts that you'll find out about job vacancies and other economic or social opportunities.

When an opportunity becomes available the first thing any employer does is examine their existing network and the networks of the other people who work there. If you are known to these people and, crucially, if they know your story (current and future) then you're in pole position to access that opportunity before it even appears in the public domain. Inside information is what it's all about. If someone is leaving the organization for a new job, or going on maternity leave . . . you want to be the first person to get a phone call.

So how do you become the person people call?

Hunt for the right people – Use Linkedin, your personal network, Twitter, Meetup.com, and any other channel to find people who work in the space you are interested in. They don't have to be recruiting managers or CEOs . . . anyone in the relevant area could give you the break you are looking for.

Build genuine relationships – Hunting for people is useless if you aren't being genuine. Be genuine by engaging in the conversation, by giving not taking, by organizing. By working for free (yes free). Emailing someone and asking them if they have any job opportunities is NOT building genuine relationships! Be generous with your introductions. Always think "how can I help this person?" rather than "what can I get out of this situation?"

Have an opinion – Natasha Malpani got her job at Big Society Capital through Escape the City, after working in a hedge fund. She says that the first thing they look at when interviewing applicants is their online presence, especially if they're transitioning into the social sector. She suggests that you write at least five intelligent blog posts that talk about your industry opinions, to demonstrate enthusiasm, genuine interest and insight. You should have a blog.

Be liked – You can't underestimate the importance of being nice. When Keith Ferrazzi talks about networking in his book *Never Eat Alone*, he talks about being liked. If people like you, they will help you. Instead of concentrating on asking for things, focus on being likeable. Otherwise, as Ferrazzi warns us, "you'll wake up when you're 40 years old in a cube and upset that a 30-year-old is your boss. And you'll say to yourself that the person got the job because the boss likes him better. And the answer will be, right."

Be trustworthy – This isn't something you can fake. You can't just appear on the scene and start expecting lots of benefit. You build trust by sharing interests with people. As soon as you're just asking someone for something it is no longer a relationship . . .

Be human – Develop genuine relationships with people who could potentially introduce you as a candidate for a new opportunity. People are opportunities. Opportunities are people. Anything you do in your career will be as a result of the people you meet along the way. Be trustworthy. Be creative. Be generous. Contribute. You get out what you put in.

Life is a series of conversations.
Conversations are networked.

Which networks are you in?
Which conversations are you a part of?

Social media relationships and personal relationships work exactly the same way — you get out of them what you put into them. You can't buy them, force them, or make them into something they're not ready to be.

Gary Vaynerchuk – The Thank You Economy

Tell a good story

The definition of a good story? "A character that wants something and overcomes conflict to get it" (borrowed from *A Million Miles in a Thousand Years* by Donald Miller).

What do you want? What stands in your way?

Humans respond well to stories. Our brains remember stories. We tell each other good stories. Your challenge is to narrate a memorable story about who you are, what you've done, and how what you've done leads into what you want to do. You should do this in applications, in person and throughout your online presence. Draw a thread through all your random past experiences and future aspirations. Show people why it makes sense (even if it doesn't necessarily!).

Help people join the dots in a compelling way and they're more likely to understand what you're looking for and refer you for the opportunities that you're after. We're also talking about the gatekeepers and connectors here, not just the end employer.

The important thing to realize is that you're constantly being interviewed for a job opportunity that you don't yet know about. You're never just assessed on the day of an interview – your reputation precedes you and your online presence represents you (or lack of it). If you can tell a story through your actions and information people can find out about you that speaks for itself (rather than having to deliver the pitch in person) all the better. What people say about you is always far more powerful than what you say about yourself.

> **66** *Ideas that spread, win.* **99**
>
> **Seth Godin – author, entrepreneur, blogger**

Own your online presence

You will be Googled. Your online presence tells a story. Own your online presence. What does your Linkedin profile say about who you are, what you're interested in and where you want to go? What does your About. me profile say, what does your CV say, what does your Twitter bio say? You can control most of the stories out there about you. What you can't control is what people say about you – but you can control all of the inputs to that process.

The traditional CV and cover letter is SO boring. Organizations want to hire people they already know and trust. Recruitment is inefficient, expensive and often fails (as in, the new hire leaves within a year). Employers want to make the process as risk-free as they can. Ask yourself how you can make yourself a safe hire for the places you'd like to work. What story can you tell with your online presence that makes people feel excited about the prospect of working with you?

What does your Escape the City profile say?!

>
> *How did you end up with this job?*
>
> *Almost any time I ask someone that question, they answer with, 'well, it's a funny story'. And it's not usually a funny story. Instead, it's a story that juxtaposes a few unlikely breaks with unadorned initiative. People get good gigs because they stand up.*
>
> **Seth Godin – Linchpin**

esc **Hunt differently**

Finding an exciting job is not an off-the-shelf process. Stop thinking transactionally. Stop spamming people with your CV and cover letter. The best opportunities never appear on a job board. Either keep applying like a mug like everyone else or start doing things differently. There is more competition today but there are also many more ways of standing out and contacting pretty much anyone you want.

Adele Barlow is Escape's fantastic Community Manager. She does an amazing job of growing our membership and engaging with the existing members to help them with their escapes and give them what they want. How did she get her job? She came to at least fifteen of our London talks and events (purely because she was interested, not because she was angling for a job). At the time she was freelancing and contracting for various digital agencies and startups. She wasn't looking for a job and we weren't hiring. However when we were in New York she ran a couple of events for us and did an excellent job. She was always in touch on the emails – introducing us to interesting people and sending through relevant articles.

When we were eventually in a position to expand the team it was a no-brainer to go straight to Adele and ask her to work with us. The opportunity never saw the light of day. Many other people had sent us speculative applications over the previous year – some specifically asking about Community Manager roles. But why would we even bother to meet someone who had just sent us an email when we had a genuine relationship built up over more than two years with someone we knew, we rated and trusted?

Adele built a relationship with Escape the City because she was fascinated by what we were building. When the opportunity arose it was obvious that she was the right person for the job and we did our best to persuade her to join us.

So if the right way to find an exciting opportunity isn't job boards, email newsletters and recruitment agencies then what is it? Firstly, you want to eliminate as much competition as you can. This means searching where other people don't, building relationships that other people aren't and positioning yourself in a way that other people can't.

Aggie Jones bagged a job at Spotify in the early days. She told us how she simply found a company that she respected and one which really excited and inspired her. However, when she looked on their website she learned that they were only hiring for a job unsuited to her experience . . . "I wrote them an email saying that although I didn't have the relevant experience for the role they were looking to fill, they simply must invite me in so that I could persuade them that I am the sort of person they would want working for them. They did, I was, and very fortunately they created a role for me!"

Martin Underwood trained as a barrister and then completed the On Purpose program. After On Purpose, he decided he wanted to work in education and technology. He wrote this blog post for us: http://blog.escapethecity.org/categories/let-the-journey-unfold/. Within a day his article received this comment: "I couldn't agree more with what you said and your experiences chime with my own. In fact, I'm now a Director of a tech startup focused on the education sector, and we're looking for someone exactly like you to join us! Feel free to get in touch – the job application is on Escape the City as of today. Would be interested in your thoughts." This led to an interview.

Be uncompromisingly yourself when you apply for jobs. If you don't want to work in an environment where you behave like a robot, don't write a cover letter like a robot. Your application shouldn't put people to sleep. It should be remarkable. It should be worth forwarding around the office. Here are two good examples of standing out:

1. Susan was fed up with wading through boring opportunities on job boards so she decided to flip the process on its head and hire her own boss. She defined her ideal boss, company and location and worked really hard to spread the word online. The result? As it was an original and creative thing to do people began spreading it. She ended up receiving 26 applications and hired two bosses.

Check out "Susan Hires A Boss" here: http://main.susanhiresaboss.com/.

2. Matt Rennie graduated into one of the worst graduate job markets the UK has ever seen. Determined to get into creative marketing, Matt made a short YouTube video explaining who he is and what he was looking for. The result? Over 10,000 views and multiple job offers. Matt ended up doing a mini tour of the UK with job interviews in Edinburgh, Newcastle, Leeds and London and even got offered a placement in New York.

Check out "A message from a graduate" here: http://www.youtube.com/watch?v=8l8FdIuYS7o.

These approaches aren't easy and there's no guarantee you'd have the same results. However, use them as inspiration to develop your own unique way of grabbing attention. If you can do this whilst telling a compelling story and building genuine relationships you'll be well on your way to finding and getting a job that excites you.

 "Great jobs, world-class jobs, jobs people kill for – those jobs don't get filled by people emailing in resumes."

Seth Godin – Linchpin

esc Interview differently

If you should write applications like a human then you definitely should interview like a real person. One of the worst things about any job is feeling like you can't bring your whole self to work. If you want to work somewhere where you can be yourself then you need to be yourself in the interview.

Remember that it is a two-way process. It is easy to focus on your nerves and the fact that you are being assessed. Remind yourself that you are judging whether you would like to work with them as much as they are you. Ask them to talk about the role and the organization's vision so you can then respond with enthusiasm. Ask punchy questions.

Interviewing is a bit like dating. If you can suggest that this job isn't your only option then people are more likely to offer you the job. If you can suggest how much the other people are going to pay you then even better. Keep your integrity though.

It's hardly believable if you claim that you're passionate about the organization just from the job description. How can you find out more about them before the interview (and tell them you've done this in the interview) to make your application more credible? No longer is it creepy to look people up online. They'll be impressed if you've done your research on them, their business plan, their press or their investors.

Once they're satisfied that you are capable of doing the job their biggest fear will be flakiness. Their biggest turn-on will be hearing that you are prepared to turn your hand to anything and that you hope that you'd be able to stay with them for the long-term and help their organization succeed. Can you offer them something valuable during the interview itself? Prepare three innovative ideas for marketing their products, developing their online presence or organizing a big event.

Don't be negative about anything you've done before. It's not impressive even if it's true and feels honest. Anyone who is going to employ you wants to believe that you're a glass-half-full person . . . additionally they want to employ someone who can spin a positive story and draw relevant themes from their past experiences.

Turn the interview into a conversation as soon as you can. Sometimes this is impossible if the person is reading from a script. But people will hire people they like. Of course you need to be competent and capable of doing the job (you wouldn't have got an interview if you weren't either of those things) but remember that the interviewer is wondering whether they want to spend five days a week with you. Make them think yes.

Actually ask for the job. It's amazing how many people never actually say this in the interview: "I really want this job, I can do this job, you can trust me to do a fantastic job." De-risk the job offer. Tell them that you'll happily work for them for a month no-strings-attached so they can see that you're capable of doing the work.

> *Don't wait for a job to be advertised. Your ideal role might not even exist yet, so you may need to make it up. There's nothing wrong with saying, 'I'd love to work for you but realize you might not have any jobs. Could I talk to you anyway?'*
>
> **Ella Heeks – became MD of organic veg box company Abel and Cole, but before she called them her job didn't exist[5]**

Conclusion – Find An Exciting Job

There is no timeframe on how long it takes to find work that's right for you. It can take years. Balancing it financially sometimes means staying in your current job or escaping and taking on a part-time job. Be patient! Go easy on yourself. Everyone seems to be in such a panic these days. You need to give yourself a break, you're not meant to have it all figured out straight away.

Through an opportunity she found on Escape the City, Alice Evans left her job as an accountant in London to volunteer at Malawian Style: "I was starting to feel that what I was doing wasn't really making a difference to myself or anyone else in the larger scheme of things." She left her internal auditor job and set off travelling, hoping to find a dream job along the way: "What I learned through this is that being an accountant isn't all that bad! There are places and companies around where you can make a difference, and where your skills are really appreciated."

Switch your mentality. Cultivate a "supplier mindset". Think not "what can I get?" but "what can I offer?" You'll learn more about yourself from a bad situation than a good one. Once you've done the hard work of creating new opportunities for yourself just pick one. Don't analyze it too much. Don't worry that you can't see around the next corner. It doesn't have to be forever. Just focus on the story that your actions are telling. Once you've chosen – remember to demonstrate commitment and determination. Don't expect to have your mind blown by how fulfilling your job is from day one. Real fulfillment comes through the process of making yourself valuable. Good luck!

> " *When you start out on a career [. . .] you have no idea what you are doing. This is great. People who know what they are doing know the rules, and know what is possible and impossible. You do not. And you should not . . .* "
>
> **Neil Gaiman – author, graduation speech – http://vimeo.com/42372767**

CHAPTER 7
ADVENTURE

We have sandwiched this chapter between the two long-term escapes (find a new job or start your own business). For most people adventure isn't a viable escape route. However, adventures (in all forms) can cause us to think dramatically differently about the world and our place in it. For that reason they're hugely valuable parts of any escape.

Many of us dream of a life that isn't ours, of freedom, and of seeing the world. However, sadly inaction often beats action. What is true for your career can also be true for your time off. It's often easier to do nothing than to do something that you really want to do that could massively benefit you.

In this chapter we talk about adventure as a metaphor for stepping outside your comfort zone. You don't have to sail around the world to qualify. By doing something outside your normal routine, you strip away the layers of your existence – your work, your commitments and your worries. We spend so much time seeing ourselves through the eyes of others that the things we are meant to discover about ourselves can stay hidden. Sometimes it requires doing something really different to unearth them.

Go on a big adventure.

 Stripped of your ordinary surroundings, your friends, your daily routines, your refrigerator full of food [. . .] you are forced into direct experience. Such direct experience inevitably makes you aware of who it is that is having the experience. That's not always comfortable, but it is always invigorating.

Michael Crichton – author

Escape the Matrix

Living in a city, working in a big company, travelling on public transport, eating hand-to-mouth (sandwiches at your desk, supermarket ready-meals in the evening), magically getting paid at the end of each month (tax deducted), wearing your uniform (a suit like everyone else) it's very easy to forget what it's like to properly look after yourself, to make your own decisions.

You can get by in this way for a long time. Forever in fact. Cruise control. Before we quit our corporate jobs adventures kept us sane. Cycling from London to Paris in under 24 hours, kayaking down a river in northern Portugal, canoeing the Yukon, road trips through California. These were distraction mechanisms for sure and we'd feel even worse when we got back to our cubicles. So why did we do this? How did it help?

We found that adventures (even quick overnight ones – walking through the night along the Sussex Downs, motorbiking in the rain to Stonehenge) helped to strip away some of the bullshit from work, society and our peers that was keeping us stuck.

Realizing that we were capable of looking after ourselves – even if it was just on a 3-day bicycle trip around northern France – is an incredibly empowering thing. If you can direct your own life even temporarily and get a thrill out of it perhaps you'll be able to consider a longer-term commitment to being fully in charge?

> "I know *exactly* what you mean. Let me tell you why you're here. You're here because you know something. What you know you can't explain, but you feel it. You've felt it your entire life, that there's something wrong with the world. You don't know what it is, but it's there, like a splinter in your mind, driving you mad. It is this feeling that has brought you to me. Do you know what I'm talking about?"
>
> **Morpheus, The Matrix,[1] Warner Brothers**

Get perspective

Matt Trinetti is an escape legend. After going through the motions of life for the past twenty-some years, he decided to take a break from working IN his life to work ON it. His first order of business: "Follow my enthusiasm and live in Europe for 7 months on my own terms." He met the Esc team in London and told us: "When I think back to my months before leaving for Europe, sometimes I felt like I was surrounded by walking dead. People who were merely going through the motions. Not hating life, but not loving it. Not living with curiosity or fire. Just plain bored."

When Mikey joined Escape the City after leaving his job in banking he headed back to his hometown, New York, to help grow Esc in the USA. He came back several times over the course of his first year and each time he commented on how exciting his new life was. Each time he returned to London he felt the juxtaposition of his new rapidly changing life in comparison to the one he'd left behind.

We are defined by our daily activity and the people in our lives. Change the context and you can change your self-definition. The benefit of spending some time travelling through a vast wilderness or living in a community that is very different from your own is that you are no longer surrounded by people you consider your peers or your competition. You are free to assess your life on its merits and based on your own values.

You don't necessarily have to quit your job, take a sabbatical, or even go on holiday to get the benefits of adventure. If you're feeling stuck or in need of a change of direction you may need to reconnect to the world beyond your immediate radius.

> *There is nothing like returning to a place that remains unchanged to find the ways in which you yourself have altered.*
>
> **Nelson Mandela**

Confront adversity

One day Paul Archer walked into work, quit his job and set off to drive to Australia in a London Taxi. Fifteen months later he arrived back in London with two World Records having done a full, previously unplanned, circumnavigation and having raised £20,000 for the British Red Cross.

"On one of the first nights of the trip, a couchsurfing host told me that you never get any good stories if everything goes according to plan. It wasn't exactly advice, but it's a great maxim to hold onto when it all goes to crap. In fact, I was in Moscow and being shoved in the dog cage of a Russian police van and heading to a Prison Cell when it came into my head and instead of feeling scared I kept thinking; 'this is going to be an AWESOME story!'. In retrospect, it was pretty terrible advice if you're concerned about your safety . . . but I did get some cracking stories!"

A few years ago Rob spent 100 days travelling through Africa from Cape Town to Cairo. At first he was driving a 30-year old Land Rover (which broke down every day) and then he was on bus, foot, train, boat and camel! The best moments were always when something unexpected happened.

Bad experiences force you to confront aspects of your character that you don't normally have to deal with in your normal life. They force you to deal with difficult situations and challenge you to react with instinct rather than standard operating procedures. You may decide that actually your life back home suits you just fine, but how are you going to know if you ever step outside your front door and head in a direction that scares you?

> **"** When everything seems to be going against you, remember that the airplane takes off against the wind, not with it. **"**
>
> *Henry Ford*

esc Plan, don't plan

It's really easy to get hung up on the details of an adventure when actually the planning can just get in the way. As with most things we've advocated in this book there are no rules! This section covers a variety of approaches that different adventure escapees have taken . . .

Don't plan

Tom Allen spent almost four years on big cycle adventures, travelling haphazardly all over Eurasia, the Middle East and Africa, and living in various cities on the way – notably Yerevan, the capital of Armenia.

> "We put together a deliberately vague route, found a few equipment sponsors in the bike industry, set a leaving date, and decided to leave the rest pretty much to chance. I decided that if I ran out of cash I would use my initiative and find a way to continue. I know that it sounds like a lot was left unplanned, and it was – deliberately. The educational value of using one's initiative to overcome obstacles and re-plan as necessary was immense, and I wouldn't have it any other way."

Spend nothing

Pete Waterman has ridden unconventional vehicles across Peru, Bolivia, India and all of North America (into the Arctic Circle). He has trained in combat sports in Thailand, travelled across Nepal and Cambodia, and raised thousands of dollars for charity.

> "I live in the middle of Washington DC and I enjoy good food, wine and beer. When I started paying attention I was shocked to realize how much I was spending on alcohol every month, from hitting bars with friends twice a week to bottles of wine at dinner on dates. I switched to showing up at happy hours with a single $20 bill for that night's drinks and started doing nice dinners more often at

home. This alone saved me nearly enough money each week to fund weeks in Asia or South America. Overall I'm lucky in that I made a great salary to begin with, but over a year and a half I saved more than half of my take-home pay by focusing on the reward of freedom, all while never really feeling I was restricting myself."

Save an adventure fund

Rob is a veteran of using automatic savings accounts for ridiculous plans. When he was 18 he and a friend decided that they'd like to drive the length of Africa one day. They promptly opened a joint bank account (much to the amusement of their friends) and started depositing something like £50 each a month into the account. Five years later they had over £5,000 saved. They bought a 40-year-old Land Rover and spent 100 days travelling from Cape Town to Cairo.

More recently, Rob and five school friends opened a savings account to fulfil a long-held dream of owning a double decker bus. This time they all set up direct debits of only £10 a week. A year later they had £3,000 in the account and they bought an old orange Bristol VR double decker bus, which they promptly named Esmerelda. For the price of a couple of drinks a week they have fulfilled a dream that they have been talking about for years!

Get funding

Alastair Vere Nicoll left his job as an associate at a magic circle law firm to become a writer and ski across Antarctica. On return he wrote a book about the experience called *Riding the Ice Wind*.

"I left the firm and got a part-time job lecturing in law. The remaining time I planned the expedition and wrote fiction. I started on a salary of less than a third of what I had been on and to begin with struggled to find extra time as preparing for lectures took more time than anticipated. In the spare time I wasn't writing, I prepared sponsorship documents, planned the expedition, put together a team and hawked my wares around the City again. Two years later we had raised £400k and I was flying in a stripped down Russian cargo plane on my way to the land that time forgot. Now that same experience has been replicated in starting my own business, for which we've currently raised around €80m."

Attract sponsorship

Paul Archer, the taxi maniac who we mentioned in the previous section, successfully got sponsorship for his trip. Probably precisely because it was such a nutty idea . . .

"Although I was saving every penny I had, without sponsorship I would have had to stick it out at my job for much, much longer to earn the required funds. We were fortunate enough to win a competition called the 'Performance Direct Non-Standard Awards', which gives money towards crazy-vehicle based endeavours, and they gave us enough funds to pay for our fuel to Australia. So off we went. We were then approached by the Taxi ordering app, Get Taxi, who challenged us and sponsored us to go the whole way back to London."

Find a grant

Dave Turner was a computer network engineer for 10 years before he became an adventure cyclist and freelance writer.

"Several months before I leave on a trip I have a good think about what it is I want to achieve. This is really important and provides a framework for me to refer to when I get mixed up. I have been lucky enough to save money from my writing, photography and my old job. The Australian Geographic Society also helps out with funds if your application is successful – this is so cool as it helps to encourage a new generation of Adventurers, Community Workers, Scientists and Research projects."

Just book a flight

Aukje is the director of RespecttheMountains.com, a freelance travel writer, and founder of beet-route.com. She recently climbed Kilimanjaro and then cycled home to Europe.

"My new partner and me were so sick of TALKING about big adventures – we wanted to DO it! Basically, we just booked tickets, put our bikes on the plane, bought what we thought we needed, planned the route to a certain extent (we had no idea where exactly we would end or where we would run out of money), and that was it. Three months later, we set foot on African soil . . . ."

Private funding

The Atlantic Rising team completed a 15-month expedition circumnavigating the Atlantic Ocean overland along the 1 metre contour line (the height scientists predict sea levels will have reached by the year 2100).

"We approached corporations and private funds with an interest in education, the environment and adventure, seeking cash or value-in-kind donations. At the peak of the recession the former was much harder to come by. We built our network of schools from scratch, cold-calling teachers until we developed a reputation and an online presence, which maintained its own momentum. We built our first website ourselves until we had raised sufficient funds to have something designed which provided a more interactive space for students and other interested parties."[2]

 Pragmatic recklessness was my philosophy.

Alastair Humphreys – cycled around the world

Adventure differently

This section shows how people have found new careers through various types of adventure and travel. These stories show how no path is the same. Sometimes finding a career you'll love can be the result of taking a small leap of faith and heading off into the unknown . . .

Sabbaticals

Sometimes taking a sabbatical can be just the thing people need to figure out what their next steps should be. Lea Woodward was one of the first people who we read about online when we were planning our own escapes.

Lea lives and works from wherever she chooses. She is an expert in the art of re-inventing yourself. She started out as a management consultant before transitioning into contract work, then re-training as a personal fitness trainer, then again as a holistic health coach and since then has had multiple ventures working on different projects all over the world.

And it all started with a sabbatical . . .

> "Sitting by my Mum's bedside and watching her die of a cancer-related complication, I realized I couldn't go back to what I knew.
>
> I decided to take a sabbatical, which then just reaffirmed what I'd been feeling for a long time. I'd never planned to stay in consulting for so long but I became stuck in the 'not knowing what else to do' (and earning lots of money) trap. As soon as I had some breathing space from the daily grind, it became obvious that I needed to do something else. So I plumped for something I thought I'd enjoy.
>
> My first escape plan turned out not to be the right thing for me but one thing has led to another (as I believe it always does when you take action) and here we are now doing my 'dream job', that I'd never really dreamed about. I hadn't dreamed about being location independent because I didn't really know the opportunity existed.
>
> We stumbled upon it when my husband was made redundant. I was convinced that we could enjoy the same standard of living on

half the cost if we just lived somewhere cheaper. So that's what we set out to do and, in the process, realized we enjoyed moving around from place to place. So far we've been to Panama, Buenos Aires, Grenada (my tropical island dream came true!), South Africa, Thailand, Dubai, Italy, HK and we are currently in Turkey."

Volunteering

After 10 years in London Jessica decided it was her time to shine, so signed up for a 6 month break volunteering in Africa to take a time-out and come up with her big idea . . . little did she know, by booking that flight . . . she had already found it.

"I was a business development and partnerships manager for a dot com in London and had worked within online marketing, partnerships and sales for the last 10 years at various high-growth (and high-tension) startups run by other people within London."

"I figured it was probably 'about my time' – but if I'm honest, Africa wasn't supposed to be THE idea – it was just supposed to be a six-month break volunteering to help me think about THE idea."

"Once the travel concept for Western Kenya came, however, I realized that through its success, I could give back much more to Africa than a few months of my time on teaching or community projects."

"Weekend one in Kisumu, Kenya, standing on top of a mountain overlooking the 2nd largest freshwater lake in the world, and miles and miles of sugar cane and rice plantations, I thought 'how the hell does no one know about this place?!'"

"I'm not exactly sure why I hadn't bitten the bullet and started something of my own before – but I think it was a combination of fear of the unknown, of failure and probably giving up my comfortable, safe standard of living."

"But living in such a poor corner of Africa and experiencing such shockingly different conditions plus all the tragedy, hope and basic necessity that comes with it has fundamentally altered my perspective on life and shot all of those fears out of the water."

Working while travelling

In 2006, Lisa chucked it all – her TV career, car, condo, boyfriend – and took off to travel and work around the world. She'd been dreaming of this most of her life and finally grabbed the chance to do it! She worked at a cafe in Melbourne, taught English in Istanbul, and volunteered in London. She started freelance travel writing and blogging . . . and the rest is history!

"For years, I'd clipped and saved articles about travelling the world or living abroad. I devoured inspirational travel narratives, and dreamed of doing it myself. Every year, I made a goal to go on one big trip. The idea didn't really ever crystallize until the year I left. My cat of 11 years had died, I ended a relationship, and while I had a great job as a TV producer, I had been growing bored with it. I realized . . . that was it. I was free and it was now or never. As soon as I reached that tipping point . . . it was like a ball rolling down hill picking up speed. Once I realized I COULD do it . . . then I knew I WOULD do it. The rest was easy."

"After four years of living out of a bag and travelling the world, I unpacked just over a year ago and have started my own Video Consulting business: LLmedia. I have combined my fifteen years of TV production experience with my online and social media skills and am helping small businesses and entrepreneurs learn how to produce videos for the web and their business. So many nowadays can shoot their own videos and I am here to help make them better. I have written an eBook chock full of tips and advice for those new to video."

"I have been taking on some speaking engagements – some encouraging others to travel (I host the Chicago portion of the Meet Plan Go movement), as well as speaking about Video at conferences like the World Travel Market in London. I also do freelance writing and photography."

Startup through adventure

James and Thom Elliot both left the London rat race to start 'Pizza Pilgrims' – selling fresh Neapolitan Pizza from a stone oven built into a three-wheeled Piaggio Ape van. In order to get inspiration for the menu, they embarked on a six week "Pizza Pilgrimage" through Italy, which was filmed for a TV show due to air in spring 2013.

We caught up with them at the start of their trip to learn more:

> "We met with a colleague, whose husband was a food critic, to chat about our plan to start a street food pizza van – and he was hugely interested and excited about it. We told him about the idea of a pilgrimage to Italy to collect our Piaggio van, and how we were hoping to film some of the trip to use as social media content."

> "He suggested that we pitch it some TV production companies and we were lucky enough to have two companies we contacted get back to us showing interest in the idea."

> "The hardest thing really has been turning our backs on a regular salary – it really takes a huge leap of faith to walk away from that. Thom proposed to his girlfriend in the same month as quitting his job, which also made it doubly hard to leave the country for a whole month."

> "The best thing about it is that feel of creating and developing your own ideas, without constantly having to look up for approval from your bosses. Seeing something that started as such a throw away idea become reality has been incredibly rewarding."

> "During the trip as well, we had our eyes opened to so many incredible Italian foods. We made pizzas for an Italian family, tasted red onion ice cream in the coastal town of Tropea and made our very own nduja, a regional spicy sausage from Calabria."

Career change through adventure

After deciding that the asset management world wasn't for her, Katherine left London and spent a year travelling around America researching for a book. She is now a writer, public speaker and the Creative Director of a young startup in New York.

> "I had wanted to be a writer for as long as I could remember. I had fallen into asset management as an interesting way to earn money

and because I felt like it was the 'sensible' option. In late 2008 I realized how stifled I felt by the life I had created and how trapped I felt by my voice. So I decided to face my fear of stuttering and change my life."

"My plan was to be the first woman to write a creative non-fiction on the experiences of those who stutter. I handed in my resignation and, a month later, moved to America to spend a year interviewing over 100 stutterers, speech therapists and researchers. No doubt I originally hoped that I would find some magical cure. Luckily I found more than I had bargained for."

"Three years later I sold my book to Simon and Schuster and *Out With It: How Stuttering Helped Me Find My Voice* became a memoir that tracked the confounding process of accepting myself and explored a uniquely human condition."

"During my year of interviews I also met and fell in love with my fiancé and joined him in launching a cell phone recycling business called ExchangeMyPhone."

"I have often felt homesick having left my friends and family in England. In creating a writing career and a business from scratch life is maddeningly stressful and nerve-racking. It is also exciting and uniquely rewarding when the gamble pays off. Travelling around the country, learning from 100 strangers, meeting my boyfriend and taking a cross-country road trip with him . . . it was the best year of my life."

Security is mostly a superstition. It does not exist in nature, nor do the children of men as a whole experience it. Avoiding danger is no safer in the long run than outright exposure. Life is either a daring adventure, or nothing.

Helen Keller – author

Conclusion – Adventure

Our lives are so full. It is extremely easy to confuse manic 'busy-ness' for fulfilment. It is important to step away from your routine to gain perspective. Every single person who has embarked on an adventure comes back changed in some way. Sometimes they return refreshed by the realization that their world isn't so bad and that a life of adventure isn't for them. Other times people come home from a trip realizing quite how stuck they had been previously.

When we were escaping the corporate treadmill, adventure helped us in two significant ways.

The first was simply a result of reading about other peoples' epic feats, listening to inspirational talks, and sometimes even meeting the adventurers themselves. Realizing that normal people are capable of amazing things was very important. From this perspective, someone else's mad adventure isn't something you have to go and do, it is simply a metaphor that you could apply to your life.

The second way in which adventure really helped us was through actually doing them ourselves. Al Humphreys talks about microadventures (experiences that are close to home, short-term and affordable – the simple act of doing things that would normally pass you by).

Between the three of us we covered a wide range of adventurous trips (none of which were worth shouting about but all of which changed us in some way): cycling through Spain, kayaking down a river in Portugal, canoeing in Canada, cycling to Paris, running along the South Downs through the night . . .

The perspective that these small experiences provided us with was invaluable. None of these trips were directly related to our escapes. But the process of making mini-escapes was a great way of upping our courage for the big one. The grass may not be any greener but you'll never know unless you look outside the cubicle wall!

> **66** *Not all those who wander are lost.* **99**
> **J. R. R. Tolkien**

CHAPTER 8

START YOUR OWN BUSINESS

This is the escape route that the three of us are most familiar with – leaving your job to build a business. The following pages cover what we have learnt from starting a business with very little experience. We want to share what you can learn from our story and how we would approach it if we were to start again.

At this point in the Escape the City story everything makes a lot more sense. However, going into it felt really scary. We had no real idea of the specifics around the business model. We simply had a hunch that building a tribe around this idea could be very valuable. We had no entrepreneurial experience, little online experience and limited money. We didn't have it all figured out but we had a clear problem that we were trying to solve. We had a mission and have worked out the details along the way.

Starting a business is many people's idea of the ultimate escape. You control when you work, what you work on and with whom. Unlike most jobs, hopefully the harder you work in your business, the more you earn. However, there is also the perception that starting your own business is a risky endeavour. Statistics get bandied around that 9 out of 10 startups fail. There are 2.4 million small business owners in the UK alone. That is a lot of people who make their living by running and owning their own thing. Don't be put off. People are building businesses all over the place.

This chapter isn't a foolproof guide to starting a business. It is a series of perspectives regarding taking the entrepreneurial route out of a professional job. You can build a business from the safety of your job or you can commit to it full-time. As with everything career and business related – there is no toolkit, there are no blueprints. You can learn from the best and still get it wrong. There are best practices and potential pitfalls. These pages attempt to summarize some of the more sensible things you could do if you're keen to try and escape by starting a business . . ..

> *If you don't build your dream, someone will hire you to build theirs.*
>
> **Tony Gaskins – author, motivational speaker**

esc Why start a business?

Ten years ago we could never have started Escape the City. Never before has entrepreneurship been so widely accessible to so many people. There has been an incredible democratization of the tools required to build a business and a vast decrease in the capital required to get a commercial venture off the ground.

This means that anyone with an idea and determination can get something started. This does not mean that anyone can be a successful entrepreneur – unfortunately commercial success is probably as hard as it always has been. You still have to create something that the market wants. You still have to avoid all the traps that young businesses can fall into.

Starting a company is your chance to build your perfect world. You get to work and play on your own terms. No more booking in a limited amount of holiday with HR far in advance. No more being held to arbitrary deadlines by senior managers. No more seeing your evenings disappear waiting for a busy partner to ask you to make formatting changes to a PowerPoint deck. THERE ARE NO RULES.

You get to work on what you want, when you want. You get to say no to some projects and yes to others. You can work till 3 am on a Monday night if you want. But equally you can take a random Wednesday morning off with no guilt. As we discuss in the following pages, it's not all sweetness and light but you do get to live life on your own terms.

Start a business because you're fed up with providing professional or financial services to another organization or individual. Start a business because you want to create something. Start a business because you want to control how you earn your living. Start a business because you want to care deeply about how you earn your living. Start a business for the sheer joy of not having to answer to a boss.

There's no rehab program for being addicted to freedom. Once you've seen what it's like on the other side, good luck trying to follow someone else's rules ever again.

Chris Guillebeau – The $100 Startup

esc **Scratch your own itch**

We spent a year before coming up with the idea for Escape the City brainstorming a whole series of frankly awful business ideas. The work-shirt rental company, the weekend hangover-recovery-kit delivery service, the bar specifically designed for talks. It was exciting but also frustrating – because we didn't feel like any of these businesses were really viable. Or at least, viable for us, with our limited business experiences and capital.

Don't worry if you can't automatically think of a business idea – or at least, any viable business ideas. What is important is that you keep generating ideas. Remember, they don't have to be something no one has thought of before. Copy the best parts of existing business models and apply them to your chosen industry, geographic area or idea. Everything is derivative in one way or another. The blogger and author James Altucher believes that you need to exercise your idea muscle – working on having ideas leads to more ideas. Check out his excellent blog post: "How to Become an Idea Machine": http://bit.ly/RckO0E.

The best advice for coming up with a business idea is "scratch your own itch". This is good advice for a variety of reasons. If you can think of a problem that you'd like a business to solve for you, the chances are other people share that problem. If you're going to design a product or service and you are the ideal customer then you'll do a better job in the early stages where many of the decisions will be hunch-based.

You don't have to be Einstein to guess where the idea for Escape the City came from. We were growing increasingly frustrated with the lack of routes out of the corporate mainstream (both job-based and startup based). We looked around us at all our fellow cubicle dwellers. Many of them looked exactly like us – 20s and 30s, good degrees, good educa-tions, ambitious and potentially extremely passionate people . . . being slowly ground down by the greyness of the corporate world.

We realized that we were far from being the only people who shared this problem and that if we were to build a business around the idea of "helping talented professionals escape big corporates" then perhaps all these people would be prepared to listen.

That's our best advice on coming up with business ideas – solve a problem. Have lots of ideas. Explore them without betting the farm. The one that keeps coming back month-after-month, that you can't stop thinking about on your way into work, is probably the one that is worth pursuing.

The reason we're so clear on what we want our business to do and whom we want to help is that we want to solve a problem that we experienced so personally ourselves. It's also why our thousands of members trust us. We're not another commission-hunting recruitment agency or salesy career gurus – our story is our member's story.

However, simply having a good idea doesn't mean that you are the right person to build it. Adele, Esc's fantastic community manager, talks about four ingredients behind any successful startup: Frustration, Conviction, Time and Skills. What frustrates you about the world so much that you'd like to fix it? What is your itch? Do you have enough conviction that this problem needs solving and that you want to be the person who builds a solution?

Adele told us how nearly every aspiring MBA student she has met wants to start a business but so few find an idea that grabs them. Even though they have the skills (and potentially the time) to start a business they are stuck if they can't identify what frustrates them. If you don't have frustration, you don't have conviction. Without conviction, you don't have momentum.

Conversely, Adele also talks about other friends who have frustration and conviction in buckets but don't have the skills to execute projects that actually address the problems that annoy them. Or, she says, they don't have the time to develop the necessary skills because they're busy working to support themselves.

Adele suggests that you let your emotional side flag your frustration and then actively convert that feeling into a conviction that you want to do something about it. Then, set aside time to develop the necessary skills.

Some people say any new business should seek to make things 1) easier, 2) cheaper or 3) more fun. Other people say your idea should sit at the intersection of "Stuff you enjoy", "Stuff you're good at", and "Stuff that people will pay you for".

We say – decide to solve a problem – the rest will follow.

> *Do something disruptive. There is no end of apps and websites that are built to be slick or super intelligent, but so many of them miss the point. Solve a real problem, have a personality, reject the status quo, be remarkable, be different, stand out, make change, learn new things . . .*
>
> **Mikey Howe – Escape the City**

Ideas are cheap, execution counts

So often we hear people saying that they would definitely quit their jobs in order to start a business if only they could come up with "that one killer idea". This is a myth. The chances are you're not going to come up with the next Cats Eye, Velcro Pad or Post-it Note. Nor do you have to invent the next Dyson hoover to come up with a good business idea.

Look around you at all the millions of businesses in your life. Copy what works. Just because you're not going to build the next Facebook doesn't mean you can't start a sensible business based on existing examples. Do something different or better (faster, cheaper or make it more entertaining). Waiting for that "one idea" is a cop out because it may never happen.

Most business models have already been thought of or are well-established. Innovate on your brand, your marketing and your message . . . but realize that your core business model doesn't have to be radically new. Escape the City is a professional social network built around a certain demographic. Sure our concept may be original but our business model is tried-and-tested.

> *It's so funny when I hear people being so protective of their ideas. To me, ideas are worth nothing unless they are executed [. . .] The most brilliant idea, with no execution, is worth $20 [. . .] I don't want to hear people's ideas. I'm not interested until I see their execution.*
>
> **Derek Sivers – founder of CD Baby**

esc Bin the business plan

The temptation to write a 50-page business plan before or while you build your business is very strong. You feel like you're being responsible, anticipating all the likely scenarios and getting a proper plan in place. You're applying all your corporate skills – you're increasing your confidence.

The problem is that every day that goes by that you're polishing bullet points in your business plan is another day that **nothing is actually changing in the outside world**. No one knows about your business. You're not testing any of your core assumptions. All you're doing is making yourself feel better. Of course plans are useful, however you can't make a real plan until you've gathered real data about the market.

You may need to get investment or land a big partnership to even get your business off the ground. You may think that these parties need to see reams of pages showing you've thought it all through. Firstly, do you want to work with people who demand this level of time wasting? Secondly, can you show them a one-page summary, a prototype, customer testimonials or some other **real proof** that you will be able to do what you claim you're going to do?

Earlier in this book we talked of the importance of applying startup thinking to your career. Here the comparison comes full circle. Instead of wasting years and lots of money finding out that your business model is flawed, adopt a "Lean Startup" approach to testing hypotheses. Develop your customers rather than your product. Apply this to your business model. Read *The Lean Startup* by Eric Ries. Get your head around the jargon. The core messages are extremely important. Heed Steve Blank's advice "no business plan survives first contact with customers" (Google "Steve Blank Udacity course" for an excellent guide through this process).

Rather than writing a business plan and pretending your way out of uncertainty you should test your way out of uncertainty. Fight the fear that stops you from putting your idea in front of the people you are building it for. You can learn so much about a potential business idea without ever opening PowerPoint.

 Your business plan is moot. You don't know what people really want until you start doing it.

Derek Sivers – Founder of CD Baby

esc Funding your startup

We're not going to dress it up; starting your own business is tough. You should know what lifestyle you are buying into before you start. Like any career path – from investment banking to charity work in Africa – building a startup comes with great benefits and some sacrifices. One of the main ones is worrying about money. You may be poor for a while and this is something you should be willing to face if you really want to do your own thing.

Below is a very brief run-down of our experiences with funding a business after escaping our corporate jobs.

It's important to remember that these are just Escape the City's experiences and understanding of funding. Feel your way. Don't get demoralized. It is a massive distraction from running your business. Rejection hurts. Speak to people but remember their advice will usually come from their own personal experiences.

Plan A – bootstrap

Stay in your job and start the business from the safety of a monthly salary. Keep saving your Escape Fund. You probably don't need any outside investment to begin with, if at all. At least if it is the type of business you can get started with minimal cash. Admittedly some businesses need significant funds to even get a prototype built but, if you can, get going without external funding.

When you start a business you have to worry about your personal bank account before you even begin thinking about the business bank account and any associated investment rounds out of which a salary could come. So first you have to answer the question "how do I fund myself" (remember our advice on "The Hit" in the Money Question). You can start a business with less than £1,000 these days. You can build a website, begin communicating your idea, start taking orders for a product that doesn't even have to exist yet.

Ultimately, the best way to fund a business on your own terms is to get someone to pay you for something and build your business organically with revenue. Being stingy helps. Starting a company today (especially online) is cheap. No office, no employees, no PR firm, no lawyers, no branding, no fluff. Do it yourself for as long as possible. Be creative. We paid for our first website with the ticket receipts from a 600-person inspirational speaker event we ran in central London.

Plan B – independent external sources

Hang on to as much equity as you can. In the long run, if the business is successful, your ownership will be worth more than the money that you sold your shares for in the early days. Obviously this isn't always possible; however, there are other ways of bringing cash into the business without giving away shares to Angels or venture capitalists.

1. **Bring new partners into the business** – Ask them to buy in. You get cash into the business and a new team member.

2. **Get a business bank loan** – We got a £20,000 Barclays Business loan at a few clicks of a button. This bought us precious months where we could expand the team.

3. **Explore incubators** – Some will give you cash in exchange for equity. You get advice, support, workspace and a peer group of fellow startups with whom you can share the ride.

4. **Hunt for grants** – There are lots of grants out there for ideas with a positive social impact (UnLtd) and governments often provide grants for high technology products.

5. **Hit up "crowdfunding"** – Get funded without giving away any equity. Kickstarter has now launched in the UK. Emilie Holmes recently raised £15,000 for her Good & Proper Tea van (helped on her way with £10 from Rob and Dom!).

6. **Friends and family** – Often the best terms you'll ever get will be from people who have known you your whole life. They are more

likely to support you at a really early stage. Make sure that there isn't scope for misunderstanding further down the line if it is an informal or oral agreement.

Plan C – Equity crowdfunding

In July 2012 Escape the City raised £600,000 from 395 of our own members by selling actual shares via a UK based platform called www.crowdcube.com. It's important to note that we brought our crowd with us. Without your own crowd this is harder to pull off. Additionally, if you have an actual business (with a brand, revenue and customers) you'll be more likely to succeed in your funding efforts.

At the time of writing there are two main providers in the UK: www.crowdcube.com and www.seedrs.com. Crowdfunding is in its infancy in the UK and the USA so you may encounter teething issues. Speak to the website owners regarding any regulatory authorizations, the process of investors depositing money into your pitch and any potential other reasons for delays.

Apparently it is important to hit the magic 40% mark when crowdfunding. Darren Westlake, Crowdcube's CEO, says that is the threshold for momentum to carry you through to 100%. Social proof and all that. Can you create scarcity around your pitch? Request pledges before you launch in order to run a queue and waiting list? Again, we acknowledge that this is tricky if you don't have a massive crowd to bring with you.

Bring non-crowd investors to your pitch if you can. This will help with that early momentum to move your pitch off the scary 0% mark. Make sure you've got your Articles and FAQs really clear. In the UK EIS and SEIS are massive tax incentives for individual private investors. We sold B shares to our crowd investors – these have exactly the same rights as A shares but they don't come with a vote at any AGMs.

Crowdcube doesn't currently allow for pre/post-money valuations. You have a single valuation on your pitch and it is the post-money one. This means that if you want to extend your round after hitting 100% the additional equity will cost you a bit more than if you were to use the pre and post-money valuation mechanism.

You need to use a crowdfunding platform in the UK because it is illegal to offer investment to the public without being FSA authorized. There are two interesting examples of companies that have raised investment in the UK without using a crowdfunding site. Trampoline Systems asked investors to self-certify as "High Net Worth Individuals" (you can read about it here: http://crowdfunding.trampolinesystems.com/). Brewdog got their investment prospectus approved by an FSA authorized account-ancy firm (you can view the pitch here: http://www.brewdog.com/equityforpunks).

We'd encourage you to try and build your business yourself first. We spent almost three years bootstrapping before we raised external capital via equity crowdfunding. Try to only seek external funding when you have pushed your business as far as you can yourself or when you have a clear roadmap for what you'd do with extra cash (if you just need it to survive then it might be a warning sign).

You can read more about our crowdfunding story here: http://www.startups.co.uk/why-one-startup-shunned-the-city-and-turned-to-the-crowd.html.

Plan Z – Venture capital/Angel investment

Don't fall into the trap of believing that this is the only way to fund a business. You're essentially committing yourself to a smaller chance of hitting a bigger prize. For every one successful VC/Angel invested company there are at least five that don't work out very well at all. And for every VC/Angel invested company there are dozens of independently owned, organically grown, responsibly run businesses.

Serious momentum is required to get a VC deal. They're looking for demos, prototypes, teams, boards, users, technology, revenue, clients and competitive advantages. They rarely fund pure ideas unless you've started successful businesses before. Not many people get VC funded.

Raising money is a massive distraction from building your business. It is very hard and can be quite demoralizing. Be prepared for this and develop thick skin. Most people won't "get it". Don't be demoralized. Just focus on increasingly clear communication.

Make sure you're not just telling the investors what they want to hear. Tell them what size of business you genuinely want to build. Big isn't better, better is better. So don't decide you need to build a £500m company unless you really want to. Define success for your company: how big, how much profit, how many employees, what valuation? Be clear on whether your vision for your company is a VC deal or not (in terms of the exits/valuations they need). You're going to have to sell a big vision to get them interested. Make sure it is your vision though.

Venture Capital is a small club and not many people get inside it. Don't get hung up on it. Try not to end up pitching. Instead ask for meetings/chats/demos/coffees. It's too easy for a formal pitch to turn into a car crash! It's a numbers game – just like job interviews. The more you do, the better you'll get. Additionally, it's also about meeting enough people until you meet someone who a) you click with and b) whose worldview aligns with your vision.

Don't jump through hoops for potential investors – create the documentation you want to show. Politely decline requests for different cuts on your information. You just don't have the time and the chances are it won't be worth it. Try not to need them. It's like dating or any cat-and-mouse game. The less you need investment the more attractive you can seem. Bootstrap, have revenue, be sustainable.

Don't obsess over the documentation (you will, we all do, but it's worth saying it!). Nail the elevator pitch: "We are going to help [this demographic] do [this]. We think the unique value in the product or service is [this feature]. We believe that we will be able to earn money [in the following ways]." Nail the plan – "This is how much we need, this is what we'll do with it, and this is what we'll have built at the end of this period."

Don't worry about negotiation. If they're good investors the valuation and percentage give-away will be fair (although watch out for the Option Pool Shuffle). "What is your valuation?" is essentially a trick question.

You're going to give away between 25% and 35% of your company and they'll either agree to fund your plan or not. The valuation is a multiple of those two figures.

Where to find investors? Introductions. Never go cold. It's a bit of a treasure hunt. Start with your network then go to Linkedin, Twitter and Angel Investment networks. Non-traditional routes include speaking to accountants, lawyers, wealth managers and fund managers. They all often have clients who might be interested in putting some of their portfolio into higher risk investments. Don't ever pay to pitch. They're the ones with the money. If you're interested in attracting Angel or VC money these sites are the best places to start learning: AVC.com, Both Sides of The Table, Angel.co, Venture Hacks.

Venture capitalists and Angel investors aren't evil but you do have to understand the game that they're playing. They want you to succeed but in order for this route to work you need to share a very clear vision. It will be a 5–7–10 year journey to boom or bust. There's less room for building a respectable sized business and you give up quite a lot of control when you sign these deals. These guys make investments into businesses that have potential to hit massive valuations. The laws of probability state that more of these investments won't hit their targets than will. You have to decide a) whether the size of your vision is a VC or Angel deal and b) whether you're up for a small chance of hitting a big prize.[1]

> *Don't worry about funding if you don't need it. Today it's cheaper to start a business than ever.*
>
> **Noah Everett – founder, Twitpic**

esc Make meaning

So you've identified the problem that your business is going to solve and you're progressing with starting up. If you're like us and have little or no money to spend on marketing and spreading the world – how on earth are you meant to make sure that the right people (your clients) hear about the business?

The answer lies in being remarkable. Heed Seth Godin's advice on standing out. Try and be a Purple Cow (the one in the field that gets noticed). "Ideas that spread, win." People don't care about your business. They care about good stories. Tell a story with your business. People will tell their friends the story of your business if it is interesting AND if the story is relevant to them. They don't care about you. They care about themselves.

Marketing used to be about broadcasting to people, interrupting them with adverts. Do you pay any attention to being interrupted these days? It is likely that brands that you feel a genuine connection with today demonstrate genuine, human characteristics. They represent a real story that you can relate to in some way. Organizations that you care about today do something that you perceive matters.

We always say that Escape the City will succeed if we can feature in the types of conversation where people complain about their jobs in the pub after work (especially since these conversations happen all the time!). This is the single most powerful reason why you're reading our book today and why people care about Escape the City. Because we've built a business that has a point, a clear goal.

What will it take for people to talk about your story in the pub? Businesses that we talk about with our friends include Threadless, 37 Signals, Toms Shoes, Zappos and Kiva. Why? Because we're fascinated by what they do, how they do it and why they do it. They have opinions. They stand for something.

Toms Shoes just sell shoes. But their motto says it all: "One pair sold = one pair donated." 37 Signals sells project management software. Subjectively boring but they write for a community of entrepreneurs, coders and designers. They recently wrote a book called *Rework* ("Change the Way You Work Forever"). They're brave enough to draw a line in the sand, pick fights and have a point of view.

The most word-of-mouth friendly businesses make meaning as well as money. Both Toms Shoes and 37 Signals make products that could be perceived as boring on the surface but people talk about these businesses. It's how I know about them and now how you know about them. Why do we talk about them? Because they're worth talking about . . ..

> *People don't buy what you do; people buy why you do it.*
>
> **Simon Sinek – Start With Why**

esc Define success

Get clear on why you are doing this. Are you trying to build a £100,000 business, a £1m business or a £100m business? Is this about making money, is it about personal freedom, or is it about solving a problem?

When we were looking for investment to fund the future of Escape the City we received a great offer from a top London VC firm. These are the kind of guys you don't say no to. It was a really tough decision. On the one hand you're in a position to say yes to something that hundreds of other entrepreneurs would kill for. On the other hand, why did we start Escape in the first place?

We reasoned that we started Escape because we valued our independence above all else. We wanted to build a sustainable, profitable business. But did we want to have to aim at a £100m valuation and then sell the business for our efforts to be defined as a success? Did we want to build Escape the City just to sell it to a big corporate? Or did we want to pursue a different definition of success?

We've constantly challenged ourselves about what "Making It" means to us. All around ourselves we've seen people ending up with the symbols of success rather than the real deal. No we haven't made millions and no we haven't finished building our business (lots still to do). Why did we quit our jobs to do our own thing? What was our original objective or definition of success? We wanted to escape to freedom and we wanted to do work that really matters to us, work we genuinely love.

Of course we wanted to earn money to afford a nice lifestyle – and we're getting there – but based on those first two tests – Freedom and Love – we're actually already there.

When you're building a business it's easy to lose sight of the small victories and the progress that you're making. The more you achieve, the more your aspirations accelerate away from you. Every now and then you have to remind yourself of your original definition of success and celebrate the small victories along the way.

Success is getting what you want. Happiness is wanting what you get.

Dale Carnegie – *author of* How to Win Friends and Influence People

esc Get going with what you've got

The temptation is always to say "oh let's just wait until we've got that bit built" or "we'll be ready when x, y or z happens". It's really important to accept that nothing is going to be perfect and you can usually always change things. Escape the City will probably never be "ready". There's always another improvement. Fight your natural perfectionism and get stuff out there. You'll fix things quicker if they're already in public.

We started a blog and started spreading the word about our concept. No idea remains unchanged by contact with the people you are building it for. The other thing to remember is that you're not really in public. In three years time with a massive customer base you'll be in public. Currently just your mum, a few friends and a couple of random Facebook fans have a clue what you're doing. So develop your idea in front of them and embrace early low-key failures. Keep the problem you're trying to solve clear but be brave enough to change tactics as you go.

Make decisions quickly. It's really hard to agonize over decisions. Sometimes they are worth agonizing over. Sometimes you need more information, advice or events need to take place in order for you to make a decision. A few things worth bearing in mind: there is rarely a "right" or "wrong" decision . . . there are just different (often multiple) paths that you could take. This is true for life as well as in business. We've found that it's far better to make a decision and get on with the plan (without looking over your shoulder) than to waste too much time trying to figure out what to do.

The sooner you can get someone to pay you the better. It doesn't matter if it's not in your world-beating business plan. As long as you have enough revenues to cover your base costs (and keep your costs really low) your business won't die. Isn't that an exciting thought?

Escape the City has made over £50,000 from hosting events over the past two years. The core of our business model has been connecting exciting organizations with talented professionals who want to do something different. However, we've always been aware that this requires lots of member data and matching technology. So we've had to develop other ways of keeping our head above water whilst we work towards our ideal business model.

So get working towards that first invoice and feel the satisfaction of not needing anyone's permission to keep going.

> *Don't let fear stop you from doing things. I had moments when I really struggled with this – I felt like my business wasn't mature or good enough. In reality, people do business with people they like, who are credible and have an enthusiasm and passion for what they do. 'Good enough' in your eyes is often 'really good' in your clients' eyes.*

Anna McKay – ex-management consultant, entrepreneur – Spinach Health & Wellbeing Ltd

esc Prepare yourself for the ride

One of the few mercies of working for someone else is that (by and large) you can switch off at the end of the day. Undoubtedly you'll have responsibilities, but usually the buck stops with someone else. Besides, you just don't care about a corporate job like you will about your business idea.

If you're mad enough to start a business you're probably in love with the idea. Be prepared to NEVER stop thinking about it! Here are some of our main bits of advice for anyone considering the entrepreneurial rollercoaster:

Protect yourself. There's so much noise around entrepreneurship it's often hard to hear your own voice. It's really important that you avoid the many distractions (conferences, blogs, twitter, email – especially email!) and get on with doing the actual work. Answering emails is not building a business. Email addiction can really derail you from doing the proper work involved with building your business. Download the Self Control App (it locks you out of the Internet for the amount of time you specify – you can't override it even if you delete the app!). Answer your emails once a day. This is the single most important productivity improvement we're working on at Escape the City.

No one will care as much as you. People will flake on you. You will care ten times more than a hired gun. Give away ownership to people who work with you. Hire fans not employees. If your startup is online find coders early doors. Working with freelancers and agencies is no substitute for developing a website in-house. There are just too many uncertainties and conversations and iterations for you to be able to build it all in one shot. If you have to keep going back to freelancers it's going to get expensive fast and will be frustratingly slow.

It's personal. We had wrongly assumed that starting a business is a professional/work-related challenge. You have an idea, you work your butt off and you try and turn it into a reality. The truth is that starting any business is a really personal experience. Try as you might, you'll identify very closely with your business. It's your baby, your idea. So when someone criticizes it or something goes wrong, you'll feel like you're being criticized or something is wrong with you. There's not much you can do here other than be aware that you'll learn as much about yourself as you will about business. And to try not to take it too personally!

Focus on viability. What would it take for YOU to define a startup as a success? Are you trying to become a one-person-business (a freelancer) or are you building something bigger than you? Is success being able to support yourself and your family? Or are you aiming at a more ambitious target? Whatever you're working towards, remind yourself of your definition of success and make sure your goals are your own. If you're not building the next Facebook don't put yourself under unnecessary pressure to hit unrealistic targets.

Evangelize selectively. Be prepared for the knocks. Use the cynics as fuel. When we started Escape we received an email from a colleague of a friend (someone we had never met). He had heard a few things about us and our business idea and took it upon himself to send us an email (no doubt well-meaning) explaining why it was a bad idea and why we weren't the right people to do it. Needless to say, it gave us plenty of motivation to keep pushing. The story of starting a business is part "take people with you" and part "ignore other people completely".

Look after yourself. It is very easy to sit at home by yourself in your pyjamas eating cereal three times a day obsessing over your new business. It's also extremely easy to go slightly crazy! Get out of the house as much as you can. Exercise, eat well and get plenty of sleep. This is right up there with the "fight email addiction" advice. Avoiding small bad habits will stand you extremely well in the long-run and help you avoid the inevitable burn-outs and lows that come with working unreasonably hard on your startup.

You'll have genuine high-five moments. In the early days of starting a business every little victory is worth celebrating. The moment you register with Companies House. The first time someone pays you for something. The first time a stranger emails you out of the blue. Your first bit of press. We personally never had moments like these in corporate land. There is nothing quite like those genuine punch-the-air moments. It feels like anything is possible.

There's no such thing as overnight success. Often people who have recently discovered Escape say to us "wow you guys have shot out of nowhere – you must be really pleased". The reality is that three years of hard graft have got us to where we are today (and there's still a very long way to go). Many businesses that you know and love today trundled along in relative obscurity for a long time before "making it". We find this reassuring. Prepare yourself for a long slog and make sure you enjoy the process enough to stick with it.

 All I can say about breaking out on your own is the highs are REALLY high, and the lows are incredibly low.

Nic Pantucci – escapee, CEO at Siasto.com, Silicon Valley

Conclusion – Start Your Own Business

It is important not to blindly evangelize startups. They are often as exciting as they sound but they are also way harder than anyone tells you. They're an extremely personal experience. We had assumed that building a business would be a work-related challenge. The reality is that the main battle is with your own psychology. However, not all startups are equal. You could decide to build a small lifestyle business that you can run from a laptop. It doesn't have to take three years and a lot of sweat and tears. Know what you're letting yourself in for and then, once you've committed, enjoy the ride!

One of the most exciting things about the 21st century so far has been the massive rise of people starting ventures with strong social objectives. Our perspective is that most people starting things today are doing it to solve a problem of one sort or another. It is really exciting that people all around the world are using the power of business to do things that matter (to them and to the world). For-profit, not-for-profit, it doesn't really matter. What venture could you start that might make the world that little bit better?

A final word on the benefits of starting a business: whether Escape the City succeeds or fails over the coming years (define success, define failure) it will have been worth it. Aside from all the obvious benefits and experiences, it will have been worth it just for the pure joy of temporarily calling the shots in our own lives. We all spend so much of our time doing what other people tell us to do.

Have you spied an opportunity to live a life on your own terms?

What are you going to do about it?

> ❝ *If you want to be useful, you can always start now, with only 1 percent of what you have in your grand vision. It'll be a humble prototype version of your grand vision, but you'll be in the game.* ❞
>
> **Derek Sivers – Anything You Want**

CHAPTER 9

THERE IS NO GUIDEBOOK

The three of us delayed our escapes by at least a year because we fell into the trap of wanting to have it all figured out. Conditioned by our education and the traditional career mentality, it was as if we were hoping for someone to tell us how to escape. If you take one thing from this book we hope it's the realization that THERE IS NO GUIDEBOOK. The magic escape toolkit doesn't exist. There is an avalanche of support and information out there if you go looking for it. Ultimately, however, you're going to have to plot your own map.

Our story is just one of hundreds of corporate professionals who have taken the time to share their transitions on our site. Reading about people who have escaped the corporate treadmill can be overwhelming. It is as if every one of them is in possession of a different secret, a secret that they know and you don't. The real secret is that there is no secret. Anyone who has built a career doing work that matters to them has had to create opportunities outside of the mainstream. Anyone whose life you admire or whose work you envy has been through the ringer. They've faced fear and uncertainty. They've failed. They've taken some risks and made some sacrifices.

A man called Joseph Campbell wrote a book called *The Hero With A Thousand Faces*. In it he explores the notion that heroic stories throughout history follow the same narrative thread, even if the story seems very different. The same is true for escapes. The stories are all different but there are certain ingredients common to all of them. If you can adopt some of these traits you'll be in a great position to create your own unique transition.

Over the following pages we've explored the themes that define "The Escapee With A Thousand Faces" and have outlined ten characteristics that you could adopt for your own escape. These are the themes that appear in almost every story where someone has rejected the status quo, society's norms and their own limited expectations for themselves. The overriding message is that it's bloody tough but that, come success or failure, it's always worth it. If you don't like uncertainty or hard work perhaps you'd be better off staying put. If it were easy then everyone would be doing it. The fact that you've read this far, however, suggests that, like us, you're also not prepared to settle. So enjoy the final chapter and then get planning!

> *Opportunity is missed by most people because it is dressed in overalls and looks like work.*
>
> **Thomas Edison**

Commit

Anyone who has achieved anything worth admiring, envying or copying has had to commit. At some point, they had to grit their teeth and turn inaction into action. They didn't necessarily have to quit their job and tell everyone they'd ever met (although sometimes that helps). But they did have to overcome their fear of the unknown and create some kind of motion in the outside world.

The surest way to force yourself to do something is to publicly commit. Once you've told all your friends that you're cycling to Rome for charity, it's hard to tell them that you're not going to do it. Once you've resigned from your job and told your boss that you're starting a mobile tea business, it would give your pride quite a knock to ask for your job back.

Start small but aim high. If someone had told us three years ago that we'd be running a business that helps people escape their jobs, with over a 100,000 members, a published book, a base in New York and a team of eight people . . . we'd have laughed at them. However, had we not committed to starting the Escape the City blog back in 2009 we never would have set ourselves on this path and you wouldn't be reading this book today.

> " *Wanted. Men for hazardous journey. Low wages. Bitter cold. Long hours of complete darkness. Safe return doubtful. Honor and recognition in the event of success.*
>
> **Ernest Shackleton – 1907, The Times**

esc **Trust the process**

Jason Fried, co-founder of 37 Signals, recently wrote a blog post called "Connecting the dots: How my opinion made it into the New York Times today"[1]. The article reads like a reverse story of his career from university onwards, starting with the moment he built his first app because he "couldn't find a simple tool to keep track of [his] growing music collection". The point wasn't to show how great he is, the point was to illustrate how lives and careers don't unfold like prepackaged Ikea furniture. Life is random, capricious and largely uncontrollable.

The only things you can control are your thoughts and actions. You never know where a new experience, project or conversation may lead. So put yourself in the right conversations and say yes to new opportunities. Since starting Esc we've seen people get job offers as a result of blog comments, we've seen people find business partners as a result of tweets, we've even seen a couple get married as a result of a conversation at one of our events (congratulations Ben and Susie Keene!). The idea for our business came as a result of a Google Image search for the keyword 'escape'.

We mentioned Steve Jobs' speech where he talked about joining the dots in reverse.[2] Now that we have been building Escape the City for three years we can join our dots up in reverse, but living it in forward motion was pretty scary. We took decisions based on instinct, driven by our values and influenced by what we learnt as we went. That's all we could do.

What does this mean? It means that you must stop trying to know what's coming next in your life. All you can do is adopt the kinds of behaviours and thoughts that just might create a future that is favourable to you. There is a huge element of faith involved in this. You cannot control the outcome. You can only control what you do today, this week and this month.

Einstein said that the definition of insanity is doing the same thing over and over again and expecting different results. Our definition of career insanity is doing work that doesn't matter to you today whilst hoping for a future full of control, autonomy and purpose. Can you see how one can't possibly lead to the other?

You'll never be absolutely certain whether a decision is right until long after you take it. Often, we stumble into our passions. Few of the most impressive career trajectories were planned in advance. Nor will yours be. Make the most of every random opportunity (especially when you're not sure of the immediate benefit to you), give more than you get and treat people well. You can't control the random chain of events so you have to trust the process.

 You can't connect the dots looking forward; you can only connect them looking backwards. So you have to trust that the dots will somehow connect in your future. You have to trust in something – your gut, destiny, life, karma, whatever.

Steve Jobs, ex-Apple CEO speaking at Stanford University

`esc` Fight fear

Confront the voice in your head. Master your psychology. Nobody has it all figured out. Almost everyone has problems and puts on a brave face – don't presume they have it easy. You see of each person what he or she lets you see. You have no idea what they are going through or what they have had to overcome to get to where they are today. Never claim that someone else "has it easy" if you don't know the entire story.

Rather than knocking them for why they can do something, why don't you have a think about why you think you can't? Chances are fear plays a large part. We don't blame you . . .

Doing something different is scary.
Quitting your job is scary.
Starting your own business is scary.
Having no income for a while is scary.
Changing jobs is scary.
Taking a point of view is scary.
Cold calling is scary.
Public speaking is scary.
Being challenged is scary.
Managing people is scary.
Saying no is scary.
Being in it for the long run is scary.
Talking to aggressive journalists is scary.

Sometimes it feels like it would be much easier to not do scary things.

Opt-out just a little bit . . .
Stay in a job you don't really like.
Coast.
Do stuff you like on the weekends.
Be able to afford nice things.
Feel OK about things overall . . . if a little unfulfilled.

It's incredibly seductive.
It's comfortable.

It's really rather nice.

Or . . .

You could use the fear as a radar.
And go straight at the things you're most scared of.

Have you got that little voice in your head saying . . .
"Wow, maybe I could do that."
"What if I could actually pull this off . . .?"

What if you listened to that voice . . . and then acted on it?
Who knows what you might achieve?

Pretty scary right?

> *If you've persuaded yourself that risk is sufficient cause for fear, and that fear is sufficient cause for worry, you're in for some long nights . . . [or] you can [. . .] realize that it's possible to have risk (a good thing) without debilitating fear or its best friend, obsessive worry.*
>
> **Seth Godin – Risk, Fear and Worry**[3]

esc Don't waste your time

Many people who lead lives that the rest of us consider too scary, risky or unrealistic use their own mortality as motivation to overcome the fear and pursue the life they want to lead.

Al Humphreys, who has spoken at all three of Escape the City's annual events in London, seems to take a morbid satisfaction in flashing up www.deathclock.com to show how many seconds he has left to live. The fact that they are counting down in front of our eyes is a particularly compelling reason to get moving on whatever kernel of a plan we're nurturing in the back of our minds.

The other technique Al uses to drive himself to build a life on his own terms away from the suffocating boredom of conventional careers is his fear of regret. In his own words: "If I have the chance to do something now and do not take it, I may always regret it."

It is the theme of death that he returns to in *There Are Other Rivers* – his account of his walk across the width of India, following a holy river.

"Each day I am one day closer to my death. No matter how aware I am of this, it is still sometimes difficult to believe in my own death." He says that, contrary to the Death Clock's predictive powers, he doesn't know when he will die . . . "so putting things off to an indeterminate date in an un-guaranteed future is pretty daft".

He is also uncompromisingly hard on himself: "There are so many interesting places I would still like to see, so many interesting people to meet, so much to do. And there is so little time. Before I know it I'll be dead and what a bloody waste of time that will be if I've just been arsing around."

As John Lennon sang in "Beautiful Boy (Darling Boy)": "Life is what happens to you while you're busy making other plans." It is far too easy to adopt a mentality of waiting and deferral. This isn't to say that we should all pursue a strategy of immediate gratification and just do whatever we want whenever we want. The point is that if you're not doing something you enjoy and all you have is a vague plan of what you will when you're "ready" in the future (when you have more money / more time / more experience / more contacts) then you are wasting your time.

Although Al Humphreys makes his living from inspirational speaking and seeks to use his exploits as a lesson in themselves, he is incredibly humble. He is also realistic. Not everyone wants to row the Atlantic and certainly most people wouldn't fancy the idea of walking a lap of the M25 motorway around London. His message is simple: "I am happiest when I have a sense of purpose."

His advice to you would undoubtedly be the same.

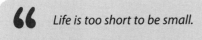

Life is too short to be small.

Benjamin Disraeli

`esc` **Reject norms**

We spend so much of our lives being told "you can't do this", "you mustn't do that". Life can often be a suffocating series of limitations and regulations. Who makes these rules? The answer is no one, everyone and you.

Norms aren't formal rules but they result in a great deal of social conformity. What we've realized since quitting our corporate jobs and building a business is that there genuinely are no rules for how you can build your career.

Advocating non-conformity for the sake of it is the career version of the moody teenager who just wants to be different. We are not encouraging petulant rebellion, we are urging you to consciously differentiate yourself from the established way of doing things precisely because the established way is unlikely to give you what you want. Fitting in may feel safe. However, in a hugely competitive job market and weak economy the surest way to become irrelevant is to keep your head down. You need to stand out. When the chips are down you don't want to be the one asking for permission.

Paul Graham, the Silicon Valley entrepreneur, startup mentor and essayist, compares graduate job-seeking behaviour to animals being let out of cages and not realizing that the door is open. We are all influenced by the cages of our existence. The fact that we aren't immediately aware of them makes them all the more effective. The belief that "the route to success is to get a good job" is so ingrained it's almost a religion. People often react to alternative advice with absolute horror. Just as they do when they hear young people being advised against going to university. These are powerful norms.

As we have repeated through this book, the past few years have shown that jobs and degrees are no guarantee of success or security. The best guarantee any working person can build to equip themselves for the future is to learn useful skills, curate a portfolio of projects and contacts and – if at all possible – build something valuable for themselves. As Graham says: "you don't have to be working for an existing company to [build something valuable]. Indeed, you can often do it better if you're not."[4]

Norms are unhelpful because they provide us with flat-pack definitions of success. The old-school business leader was driven by status, power and money. You already know that you're unlikely to be happy or fulfilled if you adopt other peoples' ideas of achievement. Belief systems are so dangerous because, by definition, they require the denial or rejection of alternative ways of thinking. Dogmatic approaches to life and work prevent us from reacting to new information and adapting to changes in our environment.

It is often said that true intelligence involves being brave enough to change your mind. We'd hazard that you're unlikely to find your own definition of success if you can't do the same.

> **"** Rules – particularly the dogmatic variety – are most useful for those who aren't confident enough to make their own damn decisions. For the rest of us, there's vodka – so we can cope with the decisions we were foolishly wise enough to make. So help us, Grey Goose. Amen. **"**
>
> *Ashley Ambirge* – **The Middle Finger Project**

`esc` Have an impact

If social norms, rules and rigid belief systems are unhelpful, then what should we use to guide our decisions? The answer lies in adopting principles. Like rules, principles are grounded in basic laws, truths or assumptions. The difference is that you choose your principle(s). You can use them as tools to guide your decisions rather than as rules for what you can and can't do. As soon as you adopt a belief system that you're not prepared to flex, you make yourself vulnerable to change – a dinosaur.

Bret Victor designed the initial user interface concepts for the iPad. He recently gave an amazing talk called "Inventing on Principle".[5] Watch it. The content is pretty technical but the core message is stunning. He talks about actively developing "guiding principles" that influence all your career decisions and give your work meaning. Specifically he explains how your guiding principles can be aimed at fixing or changing something in the world that you feel is wrong.

This isn't about saving the world (although it is often about changing it in a very specific way). Bret's particular guiding principle is a passionate belief that creators need an immediate connection to the thing that they are building. For example, he believes that when a programmer changes a line of code they should immediately see the effect of that change. This belief now informs everything Bret does. It drives him, it focuses him and it is a central reason why he is having such an impact through his work.

He warned us that it can take time to find your principle. "Finding a principle is essentially a form of self-discovery, you're trying to figure out what your life is supposed to be about. What you want to stand for as a person." He told us how it took him a decade before his principles solidified. "When I was young [. . .] I would get little glimmers of what mattered to me but no big picture. It was really unclear. This was very distressing for me. What I had to do was just do a lot of things."

The solution for Bret – as it seems to be for so many people – was to do, make and learn lots of things. Bret used a decade of experiences as a way of analyzing himself: "[I took all these experiences and asked]: 'Does this resonate with me? Does this repel me? Do I not care?' [I built] this corpus of experiences that I felt very strongly about for some reason and [tried] to make sense of it."

The Escape the City team's guiding principle is informed by the fact that so many people find working in big corporates unfulfilling. However, this alone isn't specific enough to be our guiding principle. Our specific belief is that exposure to new opportunities, likeminded people and useful information can help corporate professionals make better decisions about their future. So we've taken the broader problem and defined a specific solution that we want to work on. It is through this principle that we are seeking to have an impact.

The front cover of the *Harvard Business Review* of November 2011 carried this headline: "21st century businesses create value for society, solve the world's problems, and still make money too". If this is true for the organizations that you work in or build over the coming years then there is reason for hope both personally and in terms of the world as a whole. Working on something bigger than yourself – something related to your guiding principle – is a win-win proposition. It is the key to personal satisfaction and it is also likely to impact the world positively in some way.

If you are reading this book, you most likely have a choice in your future career path. This means you also have a responsibility to have an impact. Humankind faces some considerable challenges through your lifespan: a warming planet and a growing population are just two of the things that will impact every industry and every person through the course of this century. Do you intend for your life story to read as part of the problem or part of the solution?

 Where your talents and the needs of the world cross; there lies your vocation.

Aristotle

`esc` **Prepare for the mountain**

Starting a business is like climbing a massive mountain. In the foothills you're full of blissful ignorance and optimism. The going is often easy and you cover lots of ground quickly (after all, you're just starting out – and any momentum is more than what you had before when you were static).

You can't even see the top of the mountain at the start but you're absolutely certain you'll get there. As you continue on your journey you summit false ridges from which you see scarier ascents and bigger cliffs to climb. But the great thing is, you're also getting stronger, fitter and more experienced. So although the climbing is getting harder, you're getting better at dealing with the challenges. At the end of the day all you need to climb most mountains is determination.

Escaping the conventional career path is hard. If it were easy everyone would be doing it. You probably expect this. What you may not expect (and what we didn't anticipate) is that starting a business or changing careers is a huge emotional, personal and psychological challenge (not just a professional one).

There are big ups and downs, often not really relating to your progress but more to do with what's going on inside your head. We've been working on Escape the City for over three years. It has not been a walk in the park. It has been professionally, personally and financially challenging. It has also put us in positions we would never have been in had we carried on in the corporate groove and we've had huge amounts of fun. Mikey shared his perspective: "It is hard sometimes – but I totally knew what sort of lifestyle I was buying into when I joined you guys."

Expecting this is half the battle. It allows you to prepare. Good habits can stand you extremely well after you escape. The bottom line is that your body is capable of a huge amount if you look after it well. This means getting enough sleep, not handicapping yourself with hangovers, exercising, eating well and taking time out. We've learnt this the hard way over the past few years with a few moments of exhaustion and burnout. The irony of working harder building Escape the City than we ever did in the corporate world hasn't escaped us!

You also should remember to protect yourself – online and in person – from the barrage of advice and opinions that you'll no doubt receive if you go looking for them. All the external information can become too much. All the noise can get demoralizing. You've read everything there is to read and all you want to do is execute your plans but you're feeling stuck in a whirlpool of success stories and gurus offering their two cents' worth. When this happens just unplug from everything and carry on with your plans.

Presumably you're quitting your corporate job because you want to do work that matters to you, build something for yourself and generally appreciate life more. It is very easy to fall into your old ways of working. Make sure you enjoy yourself. If you're changing careers only change to an environment where you feel comfortable. If you're starting a business avoid simply creating another job for yourself. Give yourself a break. Work from wherever you want. Take random days off just because you can. Work all night and then sleep till lunchtime.

Escaping the city is hard but it's not impossible. Protect yourself and make sure you enjoy the ride. People escaping jobs at big corporates often joke that if they had known how hard it was going to be they might not have left.

We don't think a single one of them actually meant it.

We definitely don't.

We're pretty confident you won't either.

 I'm not telling you it is going to be easy - I'm telling you it's going to be worth it.

Art Williams – entrepreneur

Ignore cynics

If you are considering quitting your corporate job for something more exciting, unconventional or adventurous, many people will tell you that it isn't a good idea. Sometimes these people will be your nearest friends and family. They'll be naturally risk-averse because they don't want to see you in trouble (financially or otherwise). Other people will project their hopes and fears onto you if you do something different. You implicitly represent a challenge to their life choices. Expect criticism. Use this as fuel for your motivation!

Beware advice. There is an awful lot of unsolicited and bad advice out there. Advice is usually based on the experiences and worldview of the person giving the advice – not based on a real understanding of your goals. You are the only person who really knows what you are trying to achieve. When you ask people for advice they will generally tell you to do what they've done. Unless it went badly, in which case they'll tell you to do the opposite. People give you advice based on what worked for them. Not necessarily what will work for you.

The world is full of all different types of people. It's one of the reasons why life is so exciting. Optimists and pessimists, cynics and enthusiasts. When you're making any big life change you really need to surround yourself with glass-half-full people. You need all the buoyancy you can get. The tricky thing is that often those closest to you will be the ones telling you that your plans are a bad idea. There's very little you can do other than tell them that you're really excited about your plans and that you'd appreciate their support.

Illegitimi non carborundum.

> *To avoid criticism, do nothing, say nothing, and be nothing.*
>
> **Elbert Hubbard – writer, publisher, artist, philosopher**

esc **Develop three traits**

While we were writing this book we posted a series of blog posts exploring some of the core ideas in our manifesto. A chap called Toby Sims left a comment telling us how stuck he felt: "The worst part for me is finding a different path. I know I am not happy now, but have no idea where to go next." He wrote that he didn't have any particular dreams other than to "be happy". He was concerned by his lack of transferable skills ("unless you want your grass cut" – he said) and was without a life compass.

People often ask what the secret to success is. It's certainly not some trick you've never thought of. Often it's just down to a few simple behaviours. From what we've seen there are three characteristics that are extremely common amongst people who escape the corporate treadmill and transition to new paths. These are the three traits that we'd encourage to Toby to develop if he walked into our office today and repeated what he wrote on our blog:

1. Inquisitiveness – be thirsty to discover new things.

2. Bravery – be fearsome vis-à-vis rejection and failure.

3. Determination – focus like hell once you've set your goals.

From where you're sitting the thought of ever reaching the point that you're aiming at (whatever you have defined as success) can be very daunting. How many thousands of emails and millions of seconds will have to pass before you have achieved your goals? The best thing to do when you're taken over by "wow this is madness" is to focus on the next thing on your to-do list. Be determined that you will succeed in your efforts. Be brave in the face of uncertainty (you'll never "know" whether it is going to work). Be inquisitive enough to develop your skills and take new information on board that will help you on your way.

Returning to Toby's story. The same week that he posted his "cry for help" blog post he applied for and was awarded a fantastic learning opportunity on the Escape the City site. It was a scholarship for General Assembly's front-end web development 10-week evening course and it was worth almost £3,000.[6]

"Learning web development is about as far removed from my current job as it's possible to get. I'm excited because no matter how small, new skills open new doors and I can try to find an environment to flourish in rather than just exist. I'm also well out of my comfort zone, so I've got to man up. *Vive la resistance, vive l'Escape!*"

He demonstrated inquisitiveness in considering something completely new, determination in applying himself to learn a completely new skill set and bravery in putting himself out there and committing to changing his life. These traits – just like the guiding principles we discussed earlier – are so powerful because they can be applied to any career trajectory and every escape plan. As so often in life, the secret is that anyone who has achieved anything has done so through good old-fashioned graft. Are you up for it?

Things may come to those who wait, but only things left by those who hustle.

Abraham Lincoln

Conclusion – There Is No Guidebook

Our motto is "do something different" precisely because if you adopt conventional behaviours you can only hope for conventional outcomes. Think differently about your life and your career. Once you reframe the way you feel about some of this stuff you'll find it much easier to make changes that you've previously been really blocked on.

Often the harder we try to solve a problem the more the solution eludes us. Heed Einstein: "We cannot solve problems by using the same kind of thinking we used when we created them." How do we develop new kinds of thinking? How do we put ourselves in inspiration's way?

We believe that the answer is to be found in learning, experimenting and networking. Exposing yourself to new ideas, new experiences and new people is the best way of opening yourself up to new possibilities. Escapees often say they feel like fate is rewarding them for making the leap. We think the reality is far more straightforward, they are simply doing the scary work of trying new things. It is only through doing things that you can hope to discover new paths.

Well done for picking up this book and thank you for reading to the end. Use this as the spark for your escape, not the end point of your research. There is probably a year's worth of solid reading in the bibliography alone. Everything we have included in this book has helped us in one way or another. We hope that some of it helps you. As with everything, use what is helpful, discard what isn't. Take responsibility for your decisions, especially when it seems easier to blame things outside your control.

Good luck.

 You know you have only one life. You know it is a precious, extraordinary, unrepeatable thing: the product of billions of years of serendipity and evolution. So why waste it by handing it over to the living dead?

George Monbiot – journalist

A FINAL WORD

We are sitting here working through the night finishing this book. We have to submit it to the publishers tomorrow. Rob and Dom are in London, Mikey is in New York. We're listening to dance music at full volume on Spotify. Dom has just opened up the new website to a hundred test users (by now you'll have access). Eighty people are attending a sold-out Escape the City event at The Hub Westminster about starting food businesses. Our "Big Escape Picture of the Week" is being re-tweeted around the world. Things are happening.

We aren't writing this to brag, we're writing this to demonstrate how three people WHO ARE JUST THE SAME AS YOU can make things happen. Yes we didn't know it was going to work (still don't), yes we had zero cash for at least 18 months, and yes it has been an emotional rollercoaster. But every single doubt and fear is worth it when you see the results of your effort turning into real changes in the world, changes that matter to you.

Treading the conventional path is safe, it may not even be that awful, and you may be more assured of a comfortable life . . . but if you want to feel the buzz that we're feeling tonight . . . you're going to have to take that first step. Trust us, it's worth it.

There is no secret toolkit. You are the only one who can choose what comes next in your career and life. We know this is daunting; we've been there. We're with you every step of the way. You won't be taking any steps that we haven't taken already. We've survived the uncertainty and so can you.

The most important thing you can do from now on is to start taking steps in new directions. Small steps at first. If you want different out-comes you need to adopt different behaviours. We passionately believe that a meaningful existence comes from working hard on something you really believe in.

If you like what you've read, come and join us on the site. We're building the tools to help you put all of the ideas in this book into practice.

Stop Dreaming, Start Planning and Do Something Different!

All the best,
Rob, Dom and Mikey
www.escapethecity.org

PS. When you've made a transition to do something different – be it a new job, your own business or a big adventure – please drop us an email. We'd love to hear your story and share it with the rest of the community: team@escapethecity.org

> *The best time to plant a tree was forty years ago. The second best time is today.*
>
> **Proverb**

Moments[1]

If I could live again my life,
In the next – I'll try,
– to make more mistakes,
I won't try to be so perfect,
I'll be more relaxed,
I'll be more full – than I am now,
In fact, I'll take fewer things seriously,
I'll be less hygienic,
I'll take more risks,
I'll take more trips,
I'll watch more sunsets,
I'll climb more mountains,
I'll swim more rivers,
I'll go to more places – I've never been,
I'll eat more ice creams and less (lime) beans,
I'll have more real problems – and less imaginary ones,
I was one of those people who live
prudent and prolific lives –
each minute of his life,
Of course that I had moments of joy – but,
if I could go back I'll try to have only good moments,

If you don't know – that's what life is made of,
Don't lose the now!
I was one of those who never goes anywhere
without a thermometer,
without a hot-water bottle,
and without an umbrella and without a parachute,

If I could live again – I will travel light,
If I could live again – I'll try to work bare feet
at the beginning of spring till the end of autumn,
I'll ride more carts,
I'll watch more sunrises and play with more children,
If I have the life to live – but now I am 85,
– and I know that I am dying . . .

FOOTNOTES

Introduction
1. For further reading, see *The Progress Paradox: How Life Gets Better While People Feel Worse* by Gregg Easterbrook

Chapter 1
1. Black Books, Assembly Film and Television, Produced by Big Talk Productions and broadcast on Channel 4.
2. For a fascinating account of how Andreas Kluth used the inspiration of Hannibal to escape his investment banking job go to http://tinyurl.com/ax8w988
3. "Charles Leadbeater: The era of open innovation", *TEDGlobal 2005*, Posted January 2007, http://tinyurl.com/a3tewc7
4. "Robert Peston . . . life in the eye of a perfect storm", Roberts, Alison, *Evening Standard*, 4 October 2012, http://tinyurl.com/9wef3ke
5. "Crisis may be worse than Depression, Volcker says", da Costa, Pedro and Cooke, Kristina, 20 Feb 2009, http://tinyurl.com/atnaapw
6. "Wake up, gentlemen', world's top bankers warned by former Fed chairman Volcker", *The Times*, 9 December 2009, http://tinyurl.com/ahlp2ww
7. "Darling, I love you", Krugman, Paul, *The Conscience of a Liberal, New York Times*, 9 December 2009, http://tinyurl.com/a9flrqv
8. "Choose Life", Monbiot, George, www.monbiot.com, 9 June 2000, http://tinyurl.com/a26cm8f
9. "Brilliant! You won't get that high-flying job", Coren, Giles, *The Times*, 7 February 2009, http://tinyurl.com/a54gnzv
10. Read the whole William Deresiewicz lecture at http://tinyurl.com/63dzt46
11. "Alain de Botton: A kinder, gentler philosophy of success", TEDGlobal 2009, Posted July 2009, http://tinyurl.com/lnmxle
12. George Monbiot, http://tinyurl.com/3vk9syq
13. *Shawshank Redemption*, Castle Rock Entertainment, 1994

Chapter 2

1. "10 Reasons You Should Never Get a Job", www.stevepavlina.com, 21 July 2006, http://tinyurl.com/ju8za
2. "10 More Reasons You Need to Quit Your Job Right Now!", Altucher, James, http://tinyurl.com/424t289
3. Steve Jobs Stanford Commencement Speech, sourced from "'You've got to find what you love', Jobs says," *Stanford News*, 14 June 2005, http://tinyurl.com/dfbkvo or view on YouTube at http://tinyurl.com/4lxnfh
4 A Roadmap to a Life that Matters', Haque, Umair, www.hbr.org, 13 July 2011, http://tinyurl.com/69lqujq
5. "More Options, More Problems" Gulati, Daniel, *Huffington* Post, 23 June 2012, http://tinyurl.com/bhb2ugk

Chapter 3

1. "Regrets of the Dying", Ware, Bronnie, http://tinyurl.com/3956ye4
2. One Tree Hill, The CW Television Network
3. Accelerating Change, http://tinyurl.com/57fhqq
4. "Great expectations: today's babies are likely to live to 100, doctors predict", Boseley, Sarah, 2 October 2009, http://tinyurl.com/yb7akpm
5. You can read Roz's full story here http://tinyurl.com/bd53a2v and check out her amazing adventuring and environmental campaigning here: http://www.rozsavage.com/
6. *Fight Club*, Regency Enterprises, 20th Century Fox
7. "It's Not About You", Brooks, David, *New York Times*, 30 May 2011, http://tinyurl.com/b5cwczh
8. "20 Questions Worth Answering Honestly", Humphreys, Alastair, http://tinyurl.com/auc5h2v
9. "Why We Work: Finding Meaning in Your Job", by Dr Sherry Moss in Huffingtonpost.com, 2 February 2011 http://www.huffingtonpost.com/sherry-moss/find-meaning-work_b_811394.html

Chapter 4

1. "The surprising science of happiness", Gilbert, Dan, *TED2004*, Filmed February 2004, Posted September 2006, http://tinyurl.com/p2nbe9
2. "Would You Be Happier If You Were Richer? A Focusing Illusion", Kahneman, Daniel et al., *Science*, 30 June 2006, Vol. 312 no. 5782 pp. 1908–1910, http://tinyurl.com/b7gyuhp
3. *The Pursuit of Happiness*, Myers, David and Diener, Ed, Harper, 1993

4. "This Is Your Brain at the Mall: Why Shopping Makes You Feel So Good", Parker-Pope, Tara, *Wall Street Journal*, 6 December 2005, sourced from http://tinyurl.com/dynhut

5. "Seeking", Yoffe, Emily, 12 August 2009, sourced from http://tinyurl.com/acvsckq

6. Consumerism, http://tinyurl.com/ywh3ms

7. "The Epidemic of Mental Illness: Why?", Angell, Marcia, www.nybooks.com, 23 June 2011, http://tinyurl.com/3nb2z6f

8. "Kalle Lasn, founder of Adbusters, on the coming revolution", Evans, Jules, www.philosophyforlife.org, 16 June 2011, http://tinyurl.com/8yu9mha

Chapter 5

1. TED talks spreadsheet sourced from https://docs.google.com/spreadsheet/ccc?key=0AsKzpC8gYBmTcGpHbFIlLThBSzhmZkRhNm8yYIlsWGc

2. "How to Make the Leap From Corporate Prisoner to Thriving Entrepreneur", Wagner, Eric T., www.forbes.com, 21st August 2012, http://tinyurl.com/avy6uch

3. *Jerry Maguire*, TriStar Pictures, 1996

Chapter 6

1. "How To Be A Happy And Successful Creative Freelancer (Or Work With One)", Fera, Rae Ann, http://tinyurl.com/a3u9vow

2. For a discount on our workbook, go to www.startsomethingyoulove.com and enter code WELCOME1

3. "Follow a Career Passion? Let It Follow You", Newport, Cal, *New York Times*, 29 September 2012, http://tinyurl.com/aa4cfm2

4. "The Strength of Weak Ties", Granovetter, Mark, *American Journal of Sociology*, Vol 78: 6, May 1973, http://tinyurl.com/5rmhfnz

5. Ella Heeks *More To Life Than Shoes: How to Kick-start Your Career and Change Your Life*

Chapter 7

1. The Matrix, Warner Brothers, 1999

2. Tim, Lynn and Will: Warriors Against Climate Change, http://tinyurl.com/bjk7zbl

Chapter 8

1. For a full debrief of what we learnt from our VC pitching, read our blog post "Insights and Advice About Funding Startups – From Last Night's Event", http://blog.escapethecity.org, 10 July 2012, http://tinyurl.com/b8e2m2g

Chapter 9

1. "Connecting the dots: How my opinion made it into the New York Times today", Fried, Jason, http://tinyurl.com/c47went
2. Steve Jobs Stanford Commencement Speech, sourced from "'You've got to find what you love,' Jobs says", *Stanford News*, 14 June 2005, http://tinyurl.com/kwb8qq or view on YouTube at http://tinyurl.com/4lxnfh
3. "Fear, Risk and Worry", Godin, Seth, 24 July 2012, http://tinyurl.com/cydmtb9
4. "Hiring is Obsolete", Graham, Paul, May 2005, http://tinyurl.com/7gghs
5. Bret Victor: Inventing on Principle – a talk given at CUSEC 2012, http://tinyurl.com/7yf5sme
6. "Following the shiny light': Toby reports back', Sims, Toby, http://tinyurl.com/8qkagxl

A Final Word

1. This poem is often misattributed to the Argentine poet Jose Luis Borges. In recent years the poem has spread around email chain letters, acquiring something of a legendary status. The original author is still something of a mystery. We included it at the end of the manifesto as we feel it strongly reflects Escape the City's philosophy – don't fear the unknown, fear regret.

RECOMMENDED ESCAPE RESOURCES

The following resources have really helped us with our escapes. We hope some of them help you with yours.

Recommended Books

Find An Exciting Job

- *Working Identity* – Hermina Ibarra
- *Trust Agents* – Chris Brogan, Julien Smith
- *How to Find Fulfilling Work* – Roman Krznaric
- *What Colour Is Your Parachute?* – Richard Bolles
- *Drive: The Surprising Truth About What Motivates Us* – Dan Pink
- *Linchpin* – Seth Godin
- *Getting Unstuck* – Timothy Butler

Go On A Big Adventure

- *Moods of Future Joys* – Alastair Humphreys
- *There Are Other Rivers* – Alastair Humphreys
- *Walden* – Thoreau
- *The Sheltering Desert* – Henno Martin
- *The Alchemist* – Paulo Coelho
- *Vagabonding* – Ralf Potts
- *Brazilian Adventure* – Peter Fleming
- *Philosophy for Polar Explorers: What They Don't Teach You in School* – Erling Kagge
- *Life On Air* – David Attenborough

Start Your Own Business

- *The Art of the Start* – Guy Kawasaki
- *Anything You Want* – Derek Sivers
- *Start With Why* – Simon Sinek
- *ReWork* – 37 Signals
- Delivering Happiness – Tony Hsieh
- *A Book About Innocent: Our story*
- *Evil Plans* – Hugh MacLeod
- *Tribes* – Seth Godin
- *Ignore Everybody* – Hugh MacLeod
- *Crush It* – Gary Vaynerchuk
- *Purple Cow* – Seth Godin
- *From Good To Great* – Jim Collins
- *The 100$ Startup* – Chris Guillebeau
- *The Tipping Point* – Malcolm Gladwell
- *Escape From Cubicle Nation* – Pam Slim
- *4-Hour Work Week* – Timothy Ferriss
- *How They Started* – David Lester
- *Start Something That Matters* – Blake Mycoskie
- *Screw Business as Usual* – Richard Branson
- *Losing My Virginity* – Richard Branson
- *The Lean Startup* – Eric Ries
- *The E-Myth* – Michael E Gerber
- *The Long Tail* – Chris Anderson
- *Founders At Work* – Jessica Livingstone
- *Creating A World Without Poverty* – Muhammad Yunus

General Escape Advice

- *How to Change the World* – John-Paul Flintoff
- *The Dip* – Seth Godin
- *The Thank You Economy* – Gary Vaynerchuk
- *The Cluetrain Manifesto* – Levine and Locke
- *The Art of Nonconformity* – Chris Guillebeau
- *Outliers* – Malcolm Gladwell
- *The Pleasures & Sorrows of Work* – Alain de Botton

- *Status Anxiety* – Alain de Botton
- *Letters to a Young Contrarian* – Christopher Hitchens
- *The Happiness Hypothesis* – Jonathan Haidt
- *The New Capitalist Manifesto* – Umair Haque
- *I Was Blind But Now I See* – James Altucher
- *Mediated: How the Media Shape the World Around You* – Thomas de Zengotita
- *Philosophy For Life And Other Dangerous Situations* – Jules Evans
- *Here Comes Everybody* – Clay Shirky
- *What Would Google Do?* – Jeff Jarvis
- *The War of Art* – Steven Pressfield
- *How To Live: A Life Of Montaigne* – Sarah Bakewell
- *The Meaning Of The 21st Century* – James Martin
- *How To Be Free* – Tom Hodgkinson
- *What They Don't Teach You At Harvard Business School* – Mark McCormack
- *What They Teach You At Harvard Business School* - Philip Delves Broughton
- *The Seven Habits of Highly Effective People* – Steven Covey
- *Seven Day Weekend* – Ricardo Semler
- *Meditations* – Marcus Aurelius
- *On The Shortness Of Life* – Seneca
- *Whatever You Think, Think the Opposite* – Paul Arden
- *The Paradox Of Choice* – Barry Schwartz
- *Why Truth Matters* – Ophelia Benson
- *Liar's Poker* – Michael Lewis
- *An Optimists Guide To The Future* – Mark Stevenson
- *Black Swan* – Nicholas Taleb
- *What Next? Surviving The 21st Century* – Chris Patten

Recommended Articles

- Making the choice between money and meaning: http://tinyurl.com/9jh9sns
- 10 reasons you need to quit your job: http://tinyurl.com/ao4ebhr

- Choose Life: http://tinyurl.com/abhqptl
- A Brief Guide to World Domination: http://tinyurl.com/ahsn47z
- You Weren't Meant To Have A Boss: http://tinyurl.com/yp9cbl
- All of Paul Graham's articles are excellent for startup builders: http://tinyurl.com/ar4r57r
- Brainwashed: http://tinyurl.com/ax6d2nl Stop Stealing Dreams: http://tinyurl.com/au9zfbe
- Unleashing the IdeaVirus: http://tinyurl.com/bkxhxsv
- How To Become An Idea Machine: http://tinyurl.com/9448uzc
- Harnessing Entrepreneurial Manic Depression: http://tinyurl.com/4l2gpl
- Stop Asking "But How Will They Make Money?": http://tinyurl.com/9lhv7np
- The Career Value Of A Pointless Sabbatical: http://tinyurl.com/amtz6ly
- Follow a Career Passion? Let It Follow You: http://tinyurl.com/9333l7n More Options, More Problems: http://tinyurl.com/bhb2ugk
- 10 Reasons You Should Never Get A Job: http://tinyurl.com/af3wywe
- Fast Exercises To Find Your Purpose And Passion For Work: http://tinyurl.com/bxon638
- Six-Figure Businesses Built for Less Than $100: 17 Lessons Learned: http://tinyurl.com/cl8jlen

Recommended Videos

- RSA Animate – Changing Education Paradigms: http://tinyurl.com/amyzwh7
- RSA Animate – 21st Century Enlightenment: http://tinyurl.com/an65yux
- RSA Animate – Crises of Capitalism: http://tinyurl.com/b3f56el
- Elizabeth Gilbert: Your Elusive Creative Genius: http://tinyurl.com/d4tmd5
- The Last Lecture: http://tinyurl.com/52stko

- Steve Jobs' 2005 Stanford Speech: http://tinyurl.com/4lxnfh
- Alain de Botton: A Kinder, Gentler Philosophy of Success: http://tinyurl.com/lnmxle
- Simon Sinek: How Great Leaders Inspire Action: http://tinyurl.com/768kjbt
- The Corporation – Trailer: http://tinyurl.com/a6m763l
- Man On Wire: http://tinyurl.com/beyarln
- Barry Schwartz: The Paradox of Choice: http://tinyurl.com/akvzt8n
- Tony Robbins: Why We Do What We Do: http://tinyurl.com/a7oeosx
- Rory Sutherland: Life Lessons From An Ad Man: http://tinyurl.com/yfy7hn8
- Malcolm Gladwell: Choice, Happiness and Spaghetti Sauce: http://tinyurl.com/a94frph
- Jill Bolte Taylor: How It Feels To Have A Stroke: http://tinyurl.com/as5muqz
- Sir Ken Robinson: Do Schools Kill Creativity: http://tinyurl.com/bzbddct
- JK Rowling: The Fringe Benefits Of Failure: http://tinyurl.com/a3nkau
- Matt Ridley: When Ideas Have Sex: http://tinyurl.com/bzaoh7k
- Larry Smith: Why You Will Fail To Have A Great Career: http://tinyurl.com/a38w5yg
- Sheryl Sandberg: Why We Have Too Few Women Leaders: http://tinyurl.com/9weachd
- Alan Watts: Music and Life: http://tinyurl.com/be84rbw
- Alan Watts: What If Money Was No Object? http://tinyurl.com/a5custp
- Alan Watts: On Conforming To Society: http://tinyurl.com/azj5ree

ESCAPEES TO TAKE INSPIRATION FROM

Tom Allen – Tom from ride-earth.org.uk

http://escapethecity.org/users/13723/escape_story

Tom spent almost four years on big cycle adventures, living a life that is very far-removed from most of our day-to-day lives. He has some valuable (and pretty simple) advice for anyone thinking of doing something different.

Paul Archer – I quit my job to drive around the world in a black cab

http://escapethecity.org/users/42703/escape_story

One day I walked into work, quit my job and set off to drive to Australia in a London taxi. Fifteen months later I arrived back in London with two World Records having done a full, previously unplanned, circumnavigation and raised £20,000 for the British Red Cross.

Selina Barker – A career that gives me freedom and adventure

http://escapethecity.org/users/9466/escape_story

Five years ago Selina Barker quit her job as a Marketing Manager and set off to create a career that she could carry with her in a bag.

Today she is a successful online career coach, writer and adventurer – her latest adventures have had her living and working from a camper van for six months as she travelled around the UK, kayaking in Sweden, learning to surf in Costa Rica, living with artists in bohemian Buenos Aires, sailing around the remote islands of southern Chile, road tripping along the west coast of North America and hiking as many mountains and peaks as she can get her boots on. Right now you'll find her making a new home in Canada – writing, painting and getting ready for the ski season.

This is not the life she had planned – it is so much better.

Louisa Blackmore – Ex-hedge fund worker on starting out alone

http://escapethecity.org/users/3028/escape_story

Louisa escaped from the heart of the city . . . she used to work for a hedge fund and (before that) a magic circle law firm. She has recently launched her own company (selling furniture and home accessories). We'll let her tell her story herself . . .

Jessica Butcher – Kenya's "untapped gold mine of opportunity"

http://escapethecity.org/users/20266/escape_story

After ten years in London, Jessica decided it was her time to shine, so signed up for a six month break volunteering in Africa to take a time-out and come up with her big idea . . . little did she know, by booking that flight . . . she had already found it.

Piers Calvert – Exotic trader turned exotic photographer

http://escapethecity.org/users/55726/escape_story

Piers used to be an exotic equity derivatives trader at Deutsche Bank in London, but after five years he quit, leaving for South America. Today he is newly established as a photographer living in Bogotá, Colombia.

Rob Cornish – Fund manager becomes online business entrepreneur

http://escapethecity.org/users/5018/escape_story

Rob was a fund manager enjoying his work but disliking the daily regime that a job in the financial services industry entails. He escaped to a life where he works from home on the Internet and is free to work the hours he chooses.

Dave Cornthwaite – Dave Cornthwaite: skater, entrepreneur, adventurer

http://escapethecity.org/users/20/escape_story

Dave used to be a graphic designer. He left that behind and has since done some pretty crazy stuff. He is now on a mission to do lots of 1000 mile journeys around the world powered by nothing more than his muscles. He's a travel writer and a long distance skateboard record holder.

Caroline Dean – From the world of banking to founding spoonfed suppers.com

http://escapethecity.org/users/32542/escape_story

I used to work as an FX and emerging market debt salesperson in an investment bank. Then I spent some time as an investor relations and marketing associate at a global hedge fund. I started in 2005 and left in 2009.

James and Thom Elliot – 2 brothers, 1 van, and a pizza pilgrimage across Italy

http://escapethecity.org/users/85848/escape_story

James and Thom Elliot are both leaving the London rat race to start "Pizza Pilgrims", selling fresh Neapolitan Pizza from a wood fired oven built into a three-wheeled Piaggio Ape van. In order to get inspiration for the menu, they are embarking on a month-long "Pizza Pilgrimage" through Italy, which is being filmed for a TV show due to air early next year.

Nina Elvin-Jensen – From the City to my kitchen table – and littledelivery.com.

http://escapethecity.org/users/85881/escape_story

Nina set out to be successful in the City; become a professional and start working her way up the ladder to those big pay cheques. After five years as an Investment Property Agent, Nina could no longer fight a growing urge to break away from routine, the monotonous commute and big corporates. Taking one of the biggest risks in her life, she quit. And with no plan.

Adam Fenton – Corporate slave to location independent consultant and traveller

http://escapethecity.org/users/15702/escape_story

I made my escape last year when I quit my corporate IT job and bought a one-way ticket to Brazil. I spent over a year travelling through Latin America and now I'm now in the process of starting my own location independent IT consultancy (building websites and other programming jobs).

Scott Gilmore – Diplomat quits to fight poverty

http://escapethecity.org/users/85826/escape_story

Scott Gilmore was a career diplomat, frustrated by the inefficiencies of the aid industry and impatient to change them. So, he quit to launch a social enterprise called Peace Dividend Trust (now called Open Markets). Its mission: to build markets and create jobs in developing countries. It now has 150 staff working around the world. They have created over 77,000 jobs in some the world's poorest places.

Sarah Hilleary – Ex-Merrill Lynch food company owner

http://escapethecity.org/users/46/escape_story

Sarah left investment banking to start her own food company. She spotted a need in the market (something that she personally cared about) and has set out to fill it herself.

Keith Jenkins – Banking to professional travel blogger

http://escapethecity.org/users/22908/escape_story

Keith worked for 10 years in the banking world. Not sure how to escape he stalled until he saw an opportunity. He took a round the world trip and never looked back. Using his experiences in the City he built his own travel blog as a business and has never been happier.

Aggie Jones – How I got a job at Spotify

http://escapethecity.org/users/79/escape_story

Aggie so impressed her new employers when she went for a meeting with them that they created a position for her rather than miss out on the opportunity of hiring her. Nice one Aggie! Looking forward to hearing you on a Spotify ad extremely soon!

Lisa Lubin – Emmy Award winning TV producer chucks it all to travel world

http://escapethecity.org/users/46362/escape_story

In 2006, Lisa chucked it all – her TV career, car, condo, and boyfriend – and took off to travel and work around the world. She'd been dreaming of this most of her life and finally grabbed the chance to do it! She worked at a café in Melbourne, taught English in Istanbul, and volunteered in London. She started freelance travel writing and blogging . . . and the rest is history!

Dave Mayer – Former Cisco employee starts innovative hydration startup

http://escapethecity.org/users/85875/escape_story

David Mayer broke free from his corporate prison as a project manager at Cisco to start up Clean Designs LLC – an innovative water bottle company in Northern California.

Anna McKay – Anna escaped consultancy to set up a modern health company

http://escapethecity.org/users/85840/escape_story

Frustrated with the lack of modern, relevant and pro-active health services on offer by her "Big 4" company, and unable to find any companies to recommend, Anna spotted an opportunity to use her passion for sport and health to address a growing issue in the corporate world. She escaped her consultancy job to set up "Spinach", a health company tailored to the corporate world.

Matt McLuckie – Setting up sustainable carbon solutions

http://escapethecity.org/users/10284/escape_story

Eventually I decided there are two types of people in the City. In Camp 1 there are those who have long lunches and post work beers complaining about how rubbish their working life is. Camp 2 is made up of people who obviously love with passion and drive what they are doing.

Rekha Mehr – Ex-Amazon employee walks out of the jungle and into the kitchen

http://escapethecity.org/users/36602/escape_story

Rekha left her role as Buying Manager at the world's largest e-tail giant, Amazon, to start a project a little closer to her heart . . . an Indian-inspired bakery. She wanted to show that there was more to Indian sweets and desserts than is currently being offered and saw a gap in the market for a new luxury brand to step in and set up Pistachio Rose Baking Boutique.

Rob Owen – Breaking the cycle of offending

http://escapethecity.org/users/21940/escape_story

"Didn't want on my tombstone: 'Grumpy Investment Banker'." Follow Rob's transition from being an investment banker to following his passion and taking on a leadership role in an organization that is really making a difference. St Giles Trust aims to break the cycle of offending, crime and disadvantage, and create safer communities.

Nic Pantucci – If you're going to San Francisco . . . chat to Nic

http://escapethecity.org/users/20821/escape_story

My realization was sudden. On the underground while sniffing some-one's armpit for the second time that week, I decided I had to quit . . .

straight away! I presented my resignation on the day, and was in San Francisco shortly after. Think we have all been there!!!!

Trupti Patel – From Citigroup to Social Finance

http://escapethecity.org/users/2490/escape_story

After a four year stint investment banking at Citigroup Trupti found herself wondering what to do next. She now works at Social Finance, a really interesting non-profit, where she can apply her professional and financial skills to a cause she is passionate about. Thanks very much for your answers Trupti.

Katherine Preston – Katherine Preston – finance to writer and entrepreneur

http://escapethecity.org/users/15970/escape_story

After deciding that the asset management world wasn't for her, Katherine left London and spent a year travelling around America researching for a book. She is now a writer, public speaker and the Creative Director of a young startup in New York.

Steve Reid – Ex-accountant starts global sports network

http://escapethecity.org/users/85844/escape_story

After more years than I care to remember number crunching and living in MSExcel, I decided it was time to escape my humdrum accountancy day job and focus on my one main passion in life: sports. There had never been somewhere that I felt satisfied all my needs as a sports person, so I decided to build a great team and set about making Tribesports.com

Stephen Ridley – Stephen Ridley – swapping the suit for the stage!

http://escapethecity.org/users/85878/escape_story

Stephen Ridley escaped Investment Banking to be a musician: 24 hours after quitting his job, he rolled an upright piano into the middle of one of London's busiest streets and started playing. After one month he had been offered 9 management deals, and started recording his first album, "Butterfly In A Hurricane", now on iTunes.

Lee Strickland – Escape to Cornwall guest-house!

http://escapethecity.org/users/3128/escape_story

Lee and her partner are leaving the city altogether in order to head off to Cornwall and run their own guesthouse. Check out what is a brave and exciting plan. We wish you all the best guys and thanks for sharing the adventure so far. Looking forward to hearing updates.

Omar Samra – Banker quits to top Everest and start adventure travel company

http://escapethecity.org/users/85849/escape_story

Omar Samra escaped an eight year Investment Banking career at the height of the financial crisis to start a company that relies completely on discretionary spending and named it after a tropical fruit. Wild Guana-bana is an alternative take on your regular travel business. It aims at changing people's lives through travel, much in the same way travel once changed Omar's life.

Toby Sims – "There is no hope without a vision" – Toby Sims is awarded General Assembly scholarship

http://blog.escapethecity.org/categories/there-is-no-hope-without -a-vision-toby-sims-awarded-general-assembly-scholarship/

Tim, Lynn and Will – Atlantic Rising Team – Tim, Lynn and Will: warriors against climate change

http://escapethecity.org/users/15012/escape_story

Awesome adventure: "We have just returned from a 15 month expedition circumnavigating the Atlantic Ocean overland along the 1 metre contour line – that's the height scientists predict sea levels will have reached by the year 2100."

Dave Turner – Getting paid to go on cycle adventures

http://escapethecity.org/users/1448/escape_story

Dave is an Esc fan from down under – he is about to set off on an epic adventure. "I got to a stage where I just wanted to have a go at something on my own. I guess I just grew out of the rat race. It's lovely to spread your wings each day and go for it."

Aukje Van Gerven – Aukje's big risk and big adventure

http://escapethecity.org/users/20429/escape_story

Aukje is a true multi-tasker and escapee! Currently juggling three extremely worthwhile projects, this ex-administrative lawyer has finally found her calling.

Alastair Vere Nicoll – From Magic Circle to Antarctic Circle

http://escapethecity.org/users/10598/escape_story

After my first five years of professional life, I felt a little empty – as if nothing in the current circle of my existence had the capacity to truly stir me. Admittedly, to feel restless after such a comparatively short period of working life sounds somewhat pathetic. We've all felt it . . . yet Alastair is a great example of someone who has done something about it.

Jonathan Walter – Accountant becomes surfer and furniture-maker

http://escapethecity.org/users/6176/escape_story

Jonathan spent 15 years working as an accountant in an investment bank . . . "Three years ago I decided that I wanted to learn more about fine furniture, and came back to the UK, and took further studies in Devon. There hasn't been a single day of regret; I am healthier, happier, a better surfer, and way more relaxed!" Great work . . .

Pete Waterman – Pete: swapping IT for big adventures

http://escapethecity.org/users/14117/escape_story

Around three years ago, I realized I wanted to experience more outside of my career-driven lifestyle. After many experiments, I walked away from a successful career in Information Technology in early 2010 to focus on exploring the world, raising money for charity, and inspiring others through my writing and photography.

Lea Woodward – Location independent guru: Lea Woodward

http://escapethecity.org/users/85821/escape_story

Lea was one of the first people who we read about online when we were planning our own escapes. She has it sorted. She really knows what she is talking about too. Check out her answers for some nuggets of wisdom. Thanks Lea!

Frank Yeung – Burrito revolution by ex-Goldman Sachs banker

http://escapethecity.org/users/60/escape_story

Frank and Nick are true Esc Heroes and are building something really special over behind Liverpool Street. The burritos are delicious and their business acumen is pretty sharp too!

ABOUT ESCAPE THE CITY

Escape the City was born in London where Rob, Dom and Mikey were working in the heart of the corporate world – "the City". They were two management consultants and one investment banker who realised that the conventional corporate path wasn't for them. Bored and ambitious, they wanted to change but were struck by how hard it was to make the leap. Where were all the genuinely viable, exciting alternatives? It turns out that most of their friends and colleagues were struggling with the same challenge: "If not this, then what?"

What started as a simple anonymous blog has now snowballed into a service that has helped thousands of people escape unfulfilling work to find exciting new jobs, start their own businesses, and go on big adventures. Escape the City is a business but first and foremost it is a movement. The guys have assembled a community of over 100,000 corporate professionals from all around the world. The concept? A simple shared belief that life is too short to do work that doesn't matter to you.

The Esc team recently crowdfunded £600,000 investment from 395 of their own members (turning down some top venture capitalists in the process). They are hard at work building an intelligent discovery engine that helps you map your aspirations in order to connect with likeminded people and find exciting new opportunities that reflect what you really want to do with your life.

You can join the revolution at www.escapethecity.org.

ACKNOWLEDGEMENTS

We'd like to thank the people we've met since we made the leap, and the people we haven't met but who have influenced us massively online or through their books and videos.

We'd also like to thank our parents, our friends and our girlfriends. As well as the 91,657 Escape the City members who have joined the site at the time of writing and the 395 investors for believing in our vision.

We work with a fantastic team – Louisa, Adele, Fabio, Max and Kelly – the future of Escape the City would be a lot smaller without you guys.

A massive thank you to Phil Bolton, Mark Stevenson, Rob Archer, Al Humphreys, Usha Suryanarayan and Soul Patel – whose generous sharing of ideas and time have greatly influenced the book and improved it for the better.

And to those who doubt us – thanks for the added motivation!

You don't have to experience life the way you were told. The more people who wake up and realize that they have more choices than they realize, the better. The future belongs to people who are brave enough to keep pushing, obstinate enough not to settle.

INDEX

NOTES - MY ESCAPE PLAN

....
....
....
....
....
....
....
....
....
....
....
....
....
....
....
....
....
....
....
....
....
....
....
....
....
....
....
....
....
....
....

....
....
....
....
....
....
....
....
....
....
....
....
....
....
....
....
....
....
....
....
....
....
....
....
....
....
....
....
....
....
....
....
....

....
....
....
....
....
....
....
....
....
....
....
....
....
....
....
....
....
....
....
....
....
....
....
....
....
....
....
....
....
....
....
....
....